A Guide
to Retreat

A Guide
to Retreat

For All God's Shepherds

Rueben P. Job

ABINGDON PRESS

Nashville

A GUIDE TO RETREAT FOR ALL GOD'S SHEPHERDS

This book is printed on recycled, acid-free paper.

Library of Congress Cataloging-in-Publication Data

Job, Rueben P.
    A guide to retreat for all God's shepherds / Rueben P. Job.
        p.   cm.
    Includes index.
    ISBN 0-687-30270-6 (alk. paper)
    1. Retreats for clergy.   I. Title.
BV 5068.R4 J62   1994
269'.692-dc20   94-16036
                                                                        CIP

In writing original to this book, Scripture quotations, unless otherwise noted, are from the New Revised Standard Version of the Bible, copyright 1989 by the Division of Christian Education of the National Council of the Churches of Christ in the USA. Used by permission.

Scripture quotations designated AP are the author's paraphrase.

The publisher gratefully acknowledges permission to reproduce the copyrighted material appearing in this book. Credit lines for this material appear on p. 173 and following, which shall be considered a continuation of the copyright page.

ISBN 0-687-30270-6

MANUFACTURED IN THE UNITED STATES OF AMERICA

To
Beverly
who listens
for the
Good Shepherd's
voice
and
follows

CONTENTS

ACKNOWLEDGMENTS

I am grateful for all those who have been used by God to provide care for my soul. I am aware of the large number of persons who have taught me the importance of prayer, reflection, and personal retreat. To those known and unknown who have been used of God to offer guidance, nurture, and example, I offer my deepest gratitude.

I also wish to express my appreciation to friends and colleagues who gave counsel, shared their own patterns of prayer and retreat, and who encouraged me to continue this project. Special mention must be made of Janet Stephenson, Susan Ruach, David Lawson, Norman Shawchuck, Marjorie Thompson, Bruce Ough, and Jill Reddig, who responded in clear and helpful ways to my search for a retreat pattern complete enough to guide and open enough to allow creativity. Thanks also to William Cotton, Judy Smith, Jack Keller, Lovette Weems, and Susan Vogel for suggesting additional readings for the anthologies.

To the many publishers and authors whose permission has been granted for utilization of material in the text, to editors who helped me communicate more clearly, to family who tolerate my absence, and, most of all, to the gracious Source of our hunger and our food, the God seen most clearly in the face of Jesus Christ (Heb. 1:1-4), I offer my gratitude.

Rueben P. Job
Autumn, 1993

PREFACE

The house of my soul is too narrow for Thee to come in; let it be enlarged by Thee. It is in ruins. Do Thou restore it.

—Augustine

I have observed and practiced ministry for more than forty years and believe that persons in professional ministry today experience an agony of soul unlike that of any recent generation of Christian leaders. The need and opportunity for ministry multiplied, but the demands and expectations placed on ministry have grown exponentially. There was a time when the culture in this country seemed to anticipate the values and leadership embodied in the pastor and professional religious worker. That has all been changed and the current Christian worker is more like an alien in a foreign land or at least like a missionary in a mission station without adequate support.

In such an environment, pastors and other religious professionals in the church often experience disillusionment, disappointment, and depression. The contradiction between their value system, world view, and expectations and those of their environment takes a heavy toll on the satisfaction and effectiveness of ministry for many.

To sustain effective and satisfying ministry in such an environment requires an intentional effort to stay in touch with the "rivers of living water" (John 7:38) that refresh, renew, and sustain. Regular personal retreats are an important part of such an effort to keep our souls alive and healthy.

The care of the soul is a lifelong practice that is often relegated to second or even last place in our lives. We are so immersed in the demands of our noisy world that we can easily ignore the chronic emptiness deep within. That emptiness ranges from a dull ache on the edge of our awareness to a sharp pain calling all of our attention to itself. As Pascal has said, "Only God can fill a God-shaped emptiness." And only God can remove the ache of our soul.

Regular personal retreats are one effective way of creating space and time to receive God's healing for our brokenness, God's presence for our emptiness, God's companionship for our loneliness, and God's enabling strength for our ministry.

I spent the early years of my life on a farm in North Dakota. I fell in love with the prairies and with windmills. Our farm was surrounded with huge cottonwood trees that often sheltered our windmill from light breezes that would otherwise have turned it to face the wind and permitted it to do its assigned work of pumping water for the farm. When the breeze was too light to turn the huge fan into the wind, my father would climb the tall tower and physically turn the fan and tail of the windmill until it faced directly into the wind. Properly positioned, the slightest breeze was translated into life-giving water. Personal retreats can be a time of repositioning ourselves, a time of intentional turning toward God. I join Evelyn Underhill in believing that "the object of my life toward God is not . . . any personal achievement or ecstasy at all but just to make one able to do this kind of work."

INTRODUCTION

The water for which we thirst is God's grace, but God gives us the job of hauling it in our own buckets.

—Evelyn Underhill

Welcome to this time apart. *A Guide to Retreat* is designed to assist you in a time of reflection, prayer, and renewal. The resources included are intended to help you turn more fully toward God, to drink more deeply of God, and to prepare you for faithful ministry. The *Guide* is presented with the deep awareness that God is the leader of every spiritual retreat and guide of our entire life's journey. You join a multitude of persons who have discovered that a time of retreat is often the setting in which God brings new strength for ministry and new clarity, courage, and direction to life's journey.

Preparation for personal retreat will include selection of the place, time, and making the necessary arrangements for food, housing, and personal affairs while you are gone so that your time apart can be uninterrupted. It is preferable to select a location away from your regular work or dwelling place. Often space can be found in a church, retreat center, house of prayer, or even a city or state park. One of my colleagues planned regular twenty-four-hour personal retreats in a state park, winter and summer. However, if it is not possible to use a place other than your own home or office, do not let that prevent you from this intentional effort of being in God's presence and listening to God's call. If you use your own home, select a place that will permit silence and solitude. The most important thing is that you "come apart" from the distractions of your daily routine in order to hear more clearly and be more attentive to the gentle voice of the One who seeks to be your guide.

Preparations should include meals (unless you are fasting—then adequate fluids), a place to rest, and, if possible, some exercise opportunities such as walking or jogging. You will, of course, bring your Bible—and you may wish to bring a second translation to enrich your Scripture reading. Also bring a notebook and writing instrument. Upon arrival, get settled into the time and space of your retreat and consciously withdraw to this time of intimate interaction with God.

Patterns are meant to be a guide. In some instances they are to be followed without variation and in others, variation gives the pattern character and individuality. Use the pattern for this retreat in the latter sense. Listen carefully to God's voice within this retreat experience and be sensitive to how God may guide you to adjust the pattern to suit your needs for the day. While you may discard this pattern entirely at some point in the future, I encourage you to use it with only modest changes for two or three times to see whether it can indeed become a helpful model in your own spiritual journey. The points of tension you feel may be the points of growth. However, after several daylong retreats, you may be ready to modify the pattern to lead you more effectively Godward. The paragraphs that follow are intended to give some illumination on how this suggested pattern of retreat may be used.

Prayer for Guidance

The prayer for guidance can reflect your movement toward God and your invitation for God's intervention in your life. This can be a time of centering your thoughts and offering this time of retreat and yourself to the One from whom you anticipate guidance and direction and with whom you seek communion. Spend time with the printed prayer or one that you write or speak and move on only after you have placed as much of yourself and this time apart as you can into God's care and under God's direction.

Silent Listening

With a note pad near spend at least thirty minutes in quiet listening. This is a time, as Evelyn Underhill suggests, to listen for the voice of the One "who has nothing to learn from you but everything to tell you." Do not be disturbed by the many images, ideas, and feelings that flood your silence. Simply call yourself back to attentiveness to God with a brief prayer of invitation, such as, "Come, Holy Spirit," or offering, "Here I am, Lord," and continue the silent listening.

SCRIPTURE READING

Read the suggested Scripture passage several times. Try to place yourself "beneath" the passage. That is, let the passage address you with its questions and affirmations. "What is God saying to me in this passage?" Permit the passage to be God's message for you at this particular time and place in your ministry. This is not the time to seek to gather information or material for the Sunday sermon. Rather, permit the passage to be God's living Word to you. Note your feelings, questions, affirmations, and direction that come into your awareness. Plan to allow at least one uninterrupted hour for this part of your retreat.

SPIRITUAL READING

After reading the introductory essay, read one or more of the essays in the anthology. Read to hear the voice of God rather than to get information or to seek ideas. Ask what God is saying to you through this particular essay today. Allow at least one hour for this time of listening to the saints. Read slowly and reflectively, pausing for words, phrases, or ideas that capture your attention. It is all right to read only a paragraph a day if God's voice apprehends you in that paragraph.

I have made intentional effort to secure inclusive material for the anthologies. In a few instances, the value of the material was such that it prompted inclusion even though the language does not meet current expectations.

REFLECTION

Gather the notes taken during the time of silent listening, Scripture reading, and spiritual reading. Read them and note and record any common themes or messages. Allow at least one hour for reflection. Return to your notes or the readings as often as it is helpful. Record a summary of your reflection time.

MEALTIME

Light and nutritious meals can be a helpful part of your retreat experience. Receiving food with a thankful heart can be a helpful reminder of the many ways we are sustained by the abundance of God's grace. If you entered your retreat experience in the midst of a fast, you may wish to end your fast with a meal of thanksgiving during or at the end of your retreat experience. With some variation and experimentation, you will discover mealtimes to be a feast that goes far beyond food.

Rest

I have discovered that retreatants often come to a time of retreat in great need of rest. If this is true for you, feel no embarrassment about resting. An hour or two of rest or sleep may be the most important part of your retreat experience. However, if you feel a longer time is needed, or if you are consistently exhausted, it would be well to consult your physician and visit with a trusted spiritual guide.

Recreation

Follow your rest period with a time of exercise. If possible, go outdoors to walk, jog, swim, garden, chop wood, or rake leaves. Of course, do exercises that are within your capacity and are appropriate to your physical condition. If your physical activity is restricted for health reasons, an hour outdoors, even with modest activity, can be a refreshing and rewarding part of your retreat.

Journaling

Allow at least an hour to record in your journal what has been happening during this day of retreat. Once again, the notes made earlier can inform this time of writing. Note questions and directions that have surfaced. Note as well, the affirmations you have experienced and any commitments you wish to make.

Prayer

Offer your own prayers of adoration, thanksgiving, petition, intercession, and abandonment into God's care. Allow time for God to lead you in prayer with the knowledge that even when we do not know how to pray as we ought or desire, the Spirit intercedes and leads us in our life of prayer (Rom. 8:26).

Further Spiritual Reading, Reflection, and Journaling

If you have time, or wish to extend your retreat another day, continue the process of spiritual reading, reflection, journaling, and reading the Scriptures and other resources you have brought with you. You may continue in this pattern for as many consecutive days as you wish. Utilize the material in other chapters of this book, or material that you may have brought with you or may be available in your place of retreat.

EUCHARIST

Many clergy have found the celebration of the Eucharist to be a singularly formative and renewing experience while on retreat. Use the appropriate liturgy for the seasons or one that you have found to be particularly helpful and formative.

RESPONSE

While each of the stations of this retreat pattern provide opportunity for response, this is the time to focus, gather, and record your response to all that has been happening to you on this day apart. This may include a wide range of things from a simple prayer of thanksgiving to writing a new rule or way of life for yourself, or renewing commitments and covenants made in past times.

RETURNING TO THE WORLD

Many times we return from a retreat renewed and ready for our ministry only to discover that our renewed insight, vision, and spiritual energy quickly drain away. This is a time for you to consider and record the steps you intend to take to permit God to continue leading you toward maturity in Christ in your daily ministry. Refer to the appendix for suggestions about how to develop a plan for faithful living.

CLOSING PRAYER

This will be a time of thanksgiving, petition, and commitment as you prepare to return to the demands and opportunities of ministry. You may wish to use the printed prayer as part of your own personal prayer.

RETREAT  PATTERN

Prayer for Guidance

> Tender Shepherd, guide me through the hours of this retreat. Bring to my awareness your constant companionship, to my weariness your matchless strength, to my brokenness your healing touch, and to my joy your blessing. *Amen.*

Silent Listening

Scripture Reading

> Psalm 22; Psalm 23; Luke 11:1-13; Luke 18:1-8; Matthew 27:46
>
> > How does each of these passages address you today?
> > What response does each of these passages elicit?
> > What response will you make?

Spiritual Reading

Reflection

Mealtime, Rest, Recreation

Journaling

Prayer

Further Spiritual Reading, Reflection, Journaling, Prayer

Eucharist

Response: Thanksgiving, Offerings, Covenant

Returning to the World

> You may use suggestions from the appendix or design your own plan of faithful living, including daily and weekly actions designed to nurture and sustain your life and ministry.

Closing Prayer

> Grant to me, O God, the continual guidance, strength, and help of your Holy Spirit so that I may serve faithfully as your minister in your church and world. Defend and uphold me in my ministry and grant me grace to live in such a way as to please you and reflect your presence to others. Hear and accept my prayer as I offer it and my life to you in gratitude for your steadfast love. In the name of Christ. *Amen.*

1.
WHEN ALL I HEAR
IS SILENCE

*I*neffable moments are rare for most of us. The testimony of the saints confirms our own experience. While our hunger for God is universal and has been identified from the time of Adam and Eve to be our own, those peak moments of communion or union with God are extremely rare. They are there, perhaps to lure us or to reassure us, but they are not there on command or with predictable regularity. For the saints who have gone before and for us, much of life is lived out on the level plains. The plains of daily existence may be marked with deep awareness on the presence of another One who is near and who sustains, or the quiet companionship of One who guides and upholds, but there is awareness of a relationship that is life-giving.

Just as there are those peak moments of transcendence, however, there also seem to be those moments of night and silence when there is no voice of companionship and no light for our path. I say *seem to be* because theologically and rationally we declare that God is always with us. It is a truth central to our faith. In spite of the testimony of our faith and tradition and even in the face of our theology and rational declaration of God's presence with us, in spite of all of this, there are times when the reality we experience is a reality of absence, of night, and of silence. I agree with Martin Marty's assessment that "winter is a season of the heart as much as a season in the weather." Silence and absence are often a part of our life experience, as they were part of the experience of the psalmist and even of Jesus. As Jesus hung on the cross he cried out in desolation, "Why have you forsaken me?" (Matt. 27:46).

Most of us will experience these times of absence and silence in our spiritual journey. Sometimes we are so preoccupied with our own agenda we almost escape the awareness of these "dry times." Still other times, our relationship to God is so shallow that we barely notice when all we hear is silence. We become engrossed in our ministry—doing good, serving the needs of the world and of the church. But then some crisis grabs us by the throat or we are caught almost accidentally in a moment of solitude and reflection, and suddenly we are exposed. The emptiness is immense, the barrenness obvious, and the silence real.

19

In that moment, as in any other, the unthinkable may occur. The grace of assurance evaporates into nothingness and we feel forsaken and alone. Our prayers seem to go no farther than our own mind; our spiritual wells seem empty. The things that worked before no longer bring us comfort or inspiration. The assurance and confidence we once knew are gone. Our efforts to lead others become increasingly difficult and we are mocked by the silence and our own inadequacy.

A few years ago, in a period of several months, I met with nearly seven hundred pastors in groups of five to seven, for a three-hour conversation on call to ministry. One pastor said he was on "cruise control" in his ministry. He explained that, although he preached, baptized, counseled, married and buried parishioners, he had lost the sense of God's companionship, enabling presence, and guiding hand within his life and ministry. Another told of her agony of soul in trying to assure her congregation that God was present and active in their lives when she experienced such deep silence and devastating absence.

While our experiences and the description of these experiences are marked by enormous variation, many have walked this pathway before us—some for nearly a lifetime, some for a brief dark night, some for just a short stroll in the shadows when comforting voices seemed distant. We are not given the power to predict them, or how or when we will encounter such experiences, or how they will be resolved. We cannot know what prompts the silence or when it will end. We can know it is not unusual.

From the Psalms to Jesus to John of the Cross to our contemporaries there is ample testimony to the night of faith as well as testimony to the promised dawn and the silence that gives way to song. We can look to and learn from those who have gone before us. Their struggles can provide guidance for those times when the light seems so dim and the silence so complete.

Kenneth Leech candidly reports his own experiences of "unknowing" and correctly interprets St. John's "dark night of the soul" as a legitimate and to-be-expected part of the way of faith. It is often the silence that gets our attention and permits us to hear God's voice more clearly than before. Note especially the last lines of "The Sacred Silk Drum" in the anthology: "In that 'silent silken void' our daily lives will be filled—no, rather crowded and overflowing—with experiences of God."

How can we proclaim the good news of God's unconditional love when our own hearts are so empty and there seems to be no answer to our hungering cry for help? How can we lead others to the light when we feel as though we are walking in darkness? How can we stand up and encourage others to trust in God when our own lamp of faith has flickered and died? We feel it is our calling and our responsibility to point others to God. We want to walk with others until they discover for themselves that life-giving relationship with God that will see them through every experience of living and dying. We want everyone to know that intimate and sustaining relationship with God that the early church modeled and we once tasted and now long for.

At this point we may experience not only darkness but dread. As Thomas Merton said of this experience, "The more he struggles the less comfort and assurance he has, and the more powerless he sees himself to be." If you are experiencing this terrible silence, you have probably asked yourself: How can I lead the congregation? How can I model faith? Where do I go and what do I do to receive strength to go on when my source of power seems to have vanished? These are some of the questions that haunt us and often drive us to feelings of disillusionment, guilt, and even despair. If the experience is prolonged or long denied, hopelessness and deep depression may follow.

A pastor with two decades of effective ministry reported a desire to find another vocation. In conversation, he revealed the weariness he experienced in ministry when God seemed too far away. There was no sense of intimacy or companionship and to try to do Christian ministry without that presence seemed impossible.

Standing in the silence we do not need to be convinced of its reality. But we do need to be reminded of another reality. Others have travelled this way before us and their testimony, plus the memories of our own experience with our faithful Savior up to this point, assures us that we are not alone. We are given signs and songs even in the darkest night, signs and songs that assure us of the presence of the only One who can shatter our silence. When we see as Henri Nouwen does "that all that is ours is nothing, including our spirituality, and that we are totally, absolutely and without reservation dependent upon God's mercy," then our eyes are drawn away from our inadequacy to the adequacy of Jesus Christ. Even the darkness and the silence lose their fearful quality and the questions that haunt us are seen as insignificant in the light of God's mighty deeds in Jesus Christ. We begin to learn, even in the silence, that God continues to love us, guide us, and care for us.

What will emerge on the other side of silence may not be clear, but there is ample evidence that we will emerge more whole and complete than when we entered. The silence, then, is not to be feared, but embraced, for it too will pass through the strong, competent, and gentle hands of our Savior, Jesus Christ. Once we stand on the other side of this experience, we will say with the author of Romans that nothing "in all creation will be able to separate us from the love of God in Christ Jesus our Lord" (Rom. 8:39).

21

While I have never experienced the deep and extended silence of many, an unexpected illness led me to appreciate anew and to learn from the experience of others. After a busy first year as a United Methodist bishop and in the midst of an important meeting, I was awakened with shortness of breath and all the signs of problems of the heart. Soon I was in the hospital emergency room with an oxygen mask over my nose, medication dripping into one arm, and blood being drawn from an artery in the other. A team of four medical professionals was working with me and with the instruments that were monitoring my heart. I was struggling for my life.

I had so many dreams for the people of God. I had a vision of a people united in Christ who more and more reflected the Body of Christ in the world. This was the vision that beckoned me and others. But after preaching once, ordaining new clergy, and presiding for the first days of our session, I found myself in the emergency room struggling for breath. What did it mean? Who would preside over the next session? Who would preach? Where had I failed? Was this the end? Was I dying? What difference would it make? Why was I so helpless?

These questions and others plagued me as the medical team continued its efforts to control my fibrillating heart. After a couple of hours, there were encouraging signs and the medical team wanted to take my shoes off. Up to this point, they had removed the clothing from my upper body, but I remained clothed from the waist down. I asked that my shoes be left on. Finally, my wife was brought into the emergency room and she too suggested that she take off my shoes. Again I resisted, and now see it as further denial of my helplessness and dependence. Shoes became the symbol of my control, my determination, my commitment to ministry against all odds. Hours later I relented and my shoes came off.

In spite of a steady stream of visitors that prompted a "No Visitors" sign and frequent assurance of prayers and support, the questions continued. The messages of encouragement came from far and near, and with each one there was a corresponding increase in my own doubt and insecurity. Even friends began to ask, "What about your spirituality? Where is God in all of this? Why did this happen to you? Where is your spiritual vitality?"

My physical heart was gradually recovering a measure of stability, but my spiritual heart was more troubled than when I was in the emergency room. I had no easy answers for friends or for myself. Difficult days were common to my life—painful experiences had been mine as long as I could remember. But in previous times, prayers of relinquishment or abandonment were met with the healing presence that quickly blotted out the pain. Now as in the emergency room, the Jesus prayer seemed to be my only comfort and my only hope. Of course I prayed for healing, direction, strength, and light for my darkness, but nothing came clear.

In a cardiac rehabilitation program *I was taught the value of quiet times, adequate rest, meditation, prayer, and sabbath time.* How could this be? I had known all of this intellectually; I had taught these values for years. How is it that I had to be taught to remember what I knew so well? Instead of bringing encouragement and hope, this experience only deepened my despair. What was I to do? I continued to pray the Psalms and the prayers of the saints. And in response to a longing for the prairies of my birth, my wife and I drove to spend a week in the Dakotas. I took pictures of windmills against the vast expanse of sky and prairie. I watched as the invisible wind turned windmill after windmill to bring cool, fresh, life-giving water from deep in the earth. I wondered how I could position myself to catch the faintest breath of God. I wondered how the wind *(ruah)* of God could restore strength to me.

The windmill always turns to face the wind in order to catch its power and turn it into life-giving water. And, as I watched the windmills turn to face the wind, I felt myself being turned once again more fully toward God. As I felt this turning I found it possible to pray again my own prayers of abandonment and relinquishment. As I relinquished my hold on ministry, vision, and life, the depression and despair began to fade away. The voices of doubt and accusation grew more distant and the night gave way to the dawn. Spiritual reading and prayer made sense again. God's mercy and abiding presence became a part of my experience once more and the assurance of God's everlasting arms beneath me brought comfort and hope.

Was this experience the purification of the soul that others speak about? Was it the result of my action or inaction? Was it something of my own making or the result of my past? Was it simply preparation for the future, for experiences kindly hidden from my eyes? These questions continue to flash across my consciousness and while there are no simple and sure answers, there are suggestions—good ones, suggestions strong enough for us to lean our lives against without fear of falling. This guidance comes from the Scriptures and from the mothers and fathers of our faith as well as from our contemporaries. While these suggestions may not be as specific as we would like, over time they have proven trustworthy. This is guidance that can keep us going until the light appears once again, and our hearts hear and respond to the voice of God.

Your very desire to pray, to observe this day apart is not only the result of God's mercy and grace, but is also the answering response of your heart to the call of God's voice. You would not be here, you would not be yearning for God were it not for God's awakening call in your heart. Continue to ask, knock, and seek. This is a constant theme in the lives of those who have travelled the road ahead of us. Abandon yourself again and again to your faithful Savior. Open your hand and relinquish whatever it is you grasp. I refused to take off my shoes in the emergency room, refused to relinquish control to God. What is the symbol of your own pride or fear? How can you "take off your shoes" and trust God? Open your hand to receive the gift of God's companionship anew. In abandonment, silence and darkness become almost insignificant and more and more of life is trusted to God.

The rhythm of a daily rule brings order and meaning when practiced, and its memory is healing when practice becomes impossible because of illness or other circumstances. Practicing spiritual disciplines gives direction to our journey while we travel through the wilderness of wintry silence until we hear again the music of God's voice and we observe the signs of springtime in our own soul.

SPIRITUAL  READINGS

— DRY BONES —

tiredness grounds me
into a quiet stupor
of the spirit.

I yearn to be inspired,
to be lifted up, set free
beyond the place of deadness.

the struggle goes on,
however,
and you and I, God,
we exist together
with seemingly
little communion.

yet, in the deepest part of me,
I believe in you,
perhaps more strongly than ever.

I am learning you
as a God of silence,
of darkness, deep and strong.

I do not wrestle anymore
only wait, only wait,
for you to bring my dry bones
into dancing once again.

> —Joyce Rupp
> *May I Have This Dance?*

— WINTER JOURNEY: THE ABSENCE —

Winter is a season of the heart as much as it is a season in the weather. John Crowe Ransom connected the two kinds of winter:

> Two evils, monstrous either one apart,
> Possessed me, and were long and loath at going;
> A cry of Absence, Absence in the heart,
> And in the wood the furious winter blowing.

I invite the reader to undertake a journey of the soul. It will occur in the face of the threat of Absence. Some psalms will be a guide. Winter will serve as an image for the seasons of the heart.

Winterless climates there may be, but winterless souls are hard to picture. A person can count on winter in January in intemperate northern climates, or in July in their southern counterparts. Near the equator, winter is unfelt. As for the heart, however, where can one escape the chill? When death comes, when absence creates pain—then anyone can anticipate the season of cold. Winter can also blow into surprising regions of the heart when it is least expected. Such frigid assaults can overtake the spirit with the persistence of an ice age, the chronic cutting of an Arctic wind.

"Absence, Absence": a poet hears the cry. Winterly frost comes in the void left when love dies or a lover grows distant. Let a new love come into life or let the enduring one come close again, and summer can return to the heart. So it is in human affairs. The absence can also come, however, to a waste space left when the divine is distant, the sacred is remote, when God is silent. The wind of furious winter for a while blows without, and then grows silent as spring comes. The fury and the bleakness within the soul can remain, no matter what the season or the weather.

Who tends the spirit where winter takes over? The Christian faith and the family are prescribed to provide refuge and warmth, and for many they do. In our generations, however, to mention spirituality is to evoke images only of the long-day suns of summers. Those who begin with a sense of the void, the Absence, who live with dullness of soul, feel left out when others speak only of such bright spirituality.

Picture someone hungry for a warming of the spirit. He calls a friend who is advertised as spirit-filled. "Praise the Lord!" she responds, as she picks up the telephone. The two meet in person. One is chilly but open to stirrings, the other well characterized as full of stir. What transfer of spirit can occur when the filled person is compulsive about the summer and sunshine in her heart? Never does a frown cloud her face. Lips, once drawn tight in disapproval, are now drawn tight in a cosmetic smile.

"The Lord wills it." Never does the storm of a troubled heart receive its chance to be heard. The Lord has satisfied every need, one hears, so it would be a sin to stare once more at the void within. Christ is the answer, the spirit is warm and no chill is ever allowed between the boards or around the windows of the soul.

After such an encounter, questions come to mind. Is the summer-style believer being honest? Will she not have to face that void some day? Is the cry of Absence, Absence, unvoiced and unheard? Or does she ignore it? Worst of all, does she have a motive to suppress it, screen it out of her stopped ears? Does the spirit make its way only in a heart that has become a windowless hall of mirrors? Must a person, to survive, choose to create a mental sound chamber that screens out the signals of the world? . . .

For this winterward part of the pilgrimage, the authority is Karl Rahner. For a third of a century the great German thinker emitted signals to guide more than the members of the Catholic church out of which he spoke. A difficult, somewhat remote figure, he was unable to use the English language, and this limited the popularity he well deserved. Rahner instead generated a kind of trickle-down influence through seminaries and seminarians. Lay people who never knew that he helped push back the encroachments of the night and the chill still profit from what he taught their leaders. His counsel speaks across the generations.

Karl Rahner helped me grasp an understanding of two spiritual styles in an apparently casual interview held some years ago. Once upon a time there was a journal called Herder Korrespondenz, or Herder Correspondence, whose editors, fatefully for my own footnoting, did not print the date of their issues on every page. I have only the evidence, then, of a yellowed, wrinkled, often-folded, and far-faded photocopy. It dates from the days when photocopies were born gray and blurred. The top says "Interview with Karl Rahner" and the bottom, "Concluded on page 645." However, the interview loses nothing because of my inability to cite the issue that was its source or to mark the year in which it was spoken.

The interviewer had read Rahner's book *Structural Change in the Church*. "In it you say that one should test one's own faith and spirituality in intellectual solidarity with those who have perhaps excluded God from their horizon." Even translated German sounds Germanic and heavy. "Intellectual solidarity" did not mean that the believer should move to unbelief. It did mean that the unbeliever, the secular person, the modern whose horizon was not open to God, could have some valid experiences. Some of these might readily square with what the believer's heart could also feel. At least, the person of faith could "test" that faith by walking toward a horizon where God has been excluded in the eyes and senses of so many. On that horizon the furious wintry wind blows in the wood.

The interviewer asked, "Is that the point at which the Church of the future can find new motivations?" One pictures the short, stern-looking Rahner, scowling behind his glasses, being deliberate, as always: "Really, I don't know how to answer that question." And then Rahner answered it brilliantly. "I am inclined to think that in the future there will be two types of spirituality and piety—naturally they are related to each other and, once again, are not chemically pure." In matters of faith and piety, nothing is ever chemically pure. The summery types have to be honest and know that behind their smiling façades and their forced Praise the Lords the serious soul knows Absence when doubt pleads for time, when despair intrudes, when death scourges. And what of the wintry persons who test faith in solidarity with those on the godless horizon? They will not endure if they *never* can respond with a Yes. Such seekers will not wait for God forever, unless some warm rays of affirmation break through the winter in their hearts. No, the two types are not "chemically pure."

—Martin E. Marty
A Cry of Absence

— THE SACRED SILK DRUM —

Once upon a time, long ago in ancient Japan, there lived a mighty lord who realized that his death was very near. He urged his only daughter, the Lady Yumiyo, that she should marry. He said to her, "Dearest daughter, the green of the plum trees has come and gone and it is the time of the blossoms. But you, dear one, still have not chosen a husband. All those men who have come for your hand you have dismissed. Am I, your father, to die without seeing you married and without seeing my grandchildren?"

His daughter replied, "No, father, for I shall fashion a drum of silk which will be stretched over a bamboo frame. The man who hears the note when my fingers strike the drum, that man will I marry."

"What foolishness!" said the old man. "A silk drum does not make any sound. Poor me, I shall die without seeing my grandchildren." But the Lady Yumiyo was as strong-willed as she was beautiful, and so the silk drum was made. Many young men came to listen to her drum, because she was not only beautiful but also very rich. But, alas, when she played upon her silk drum not a sound did any of them hear. The months and seasons passed, as a long procession of suitors came and went. The aged lord mumbled, "Oh, I told you so, I told you so!"

Then one day, into the courtyard came a young, handsome and richly-dressed man. He had about him the air of one who had traveled long and far. He made a deep bow to the aged lord and a lesser but gentle one to the Lady Yumiyo who sat with her silk drum at her side.

"From where do you come, youthful stranger?" asked the father.

"From beyond the mountains and the seas; from far, far away," replied the youthful stranger.

"And for what, may I ask, have you traveled such a great distance?" asked the father.

"My Lord," said the young man, "I have come to marry your daughter."

"She is only for the man who can hear her silk drum. Do not tell me that you have heard its sound in your far-off kingdom, across the mountains and the seas?"

The young man answered, "You are correct, my Lord, no sound of the drum has reached me."

"Then, stranger," said the father, "be on your way, like all the others before you. Why do you even linger here?"

"Because, my Lord," said the young stranger, "I hear its silence."

And the Lady Yumiyo smiled and put away her silken drum, since she had no further use for it.

The Samaritan in the story that was told by Jesus heard a silken drum. Its sound is the absence of all sound. It can be heard not only across vast mountain ranges and seas, but even beyond time and space! Those who hear the silk drum of heaven do indeed, as Henry Thoreau said, keep a different pace than their companions. But you and I, like the frustrated suitors in the old Japanese story, are eager to love God and strain our ears to hear a divine voice. And when we fail to hear anything, when we fail to see anything, we express our religious dilemma and are told, "You must have faith. You must learn to believe in that which you cannot see, touch or hear." Such pious-sounding advice only sets our feet to an arid pathway. For how can we ever learn to love with such a totality of energy—with all our heart, all our soul and all our strength—*unless* we do hear, see and feel? Can we, like the young stranger in the old Japanese story, hear the "silence" of the sacred silk drum? Can we hear the voice of God in its very silence? Can we feel the intimate touch of the Divine Lover in the presence of every touch?

If we desire to love with such a totality and to express that love by living in prayerful unity with the Divine Mystery, then two things will be necessary. First, we will keep in mind that the God we believe in is the God we will experience. For example, if we believe in a God who is a strict judge, an almighty judge who acts like some character from a

Charles Dickens' novel who punishes his children so that they will be good, then that will be the God we will experience. That will be the God we will pray to for mercy and forgiveness. As a result of such a belief, our lives will be measured by the drumbeat of laws, regulations and obligations. We will live in fear, and our prayer will be that of pleading for mercy. Or, if we believe that the Divine Presence speaks to us in a fiery volcanic voice or in shimmering lights in the night, then we will never hear the "real" voice of our God. But, if we believe that God does indeed play upon a silken drum, plays upon it with a lover's fingers, then the strongest proof for the existence of God will be the absence of God! And then, in that "silent, silken void," our daily lives will be filled—no, rather crowded and overflowing—with experiences of God.

—Edward Hays
Pray All Ways

— WHEN GOD SEEMS ABSENT —

This feeling of absence of God's presence, this dryness of the spirit, is not evil. It is not something to dread and fight against. Some people advise just restful quiescence, peaceful waiting for the spiritual winds to blow and the fog to lift. For myself, I suggest a more active, alert response. The following suggestions for the renewal of our awareness of God's closeness are not the same as contrivance of appropriate feelings, but they do seem to help clear the space, prepare the way, attune our attentiveness, heighten our sensitive response to God, who loves us.

Perhaps the best place to be in is to search our lives for any condition that is draining us, feeding on our vitality, lowering our energy to the point that it is hard to feel anything. . . . You may well find a connection between inner exhaustion and the loss of the awareness of God's closeness.

Another place to look is at our unhealed wounds, the traumatized trust, the unclear anger, the submerged grieving. Such wounds can surface unexpectedly and blot out the light of God for us. . . .

A third suggestion is to try new ways of praying, relating to God, not grimly as if to force a feeling, but with expectancy and anticipation. You may wish to try alternating between a regular, intentional time of prayer and a more spontaneous approach. You will move from one to the other with refreshed joy. It is deadening (for me, anyway) to pray the same way all the time.

Let your body help you. Our bodies will be spiritual guides and friends if we will let them. Our bodies are in touch with our deep subconscious selves, through which God speaks more clearly than to our conscious minds.

For example, let your body move during prayer if that feels comfortable to you. You may want to walk around, kneel, take a few dance steps, stretch, hug yourself, raise your arms, lay loving, healing hands on yourself. You may want to sing, laugh, cry, speak aloud certain words or phrases.

Or you may want to take what I call a "parable walk," in which you take a walk without an agenda and see what God is personally telling you through the shape of a tree, a cloud, a dog, an ant, a bird, someone's face, a window, a color, a fragrance, a touch, a sound. There is always something you will experience, no matter in how small a way, which has significance for you.

Or you may want to write a letter to God, a totally honest letter, as you would write to the friend you trust most. Tell everything you feel in this letter to God, including your doubts about God and your anger.

Or set a chair in front of you, and ask Jesus, the Risen One, to sit there. Talk to him, inwardly or aloud, sharing your needs and feelings and longings. Then sit silently and see what seems to come to you inwardly. If nothing seems to happen at this time, keep alert the next few hours and days to see what changes come into your life. Usually what happens is very unexpected.

While you pray or meditate, hold in your hands a special picture or object that reminds you of God. Holding it against your heart may be a powerful experience. A friend once loaned me a beautiful copy of an Eastern Orthodox icon. (These can be found in many religious bookstores.) I laid it against my heart and just sat quietly, not picturing or asking anything. I was astounded at the river of energy and love that seemed to flow into my heart from the picture of the Christ. There came a feeling of direct communication that I had not experienced in many months. Such pictures are looked upon, by those who paint and pray with them, as open windows through which we look at God and God looks back at us.

But the object you hold need not necessarily be a picture. It can be a book, a cross, a pebble, a flower, a piece of cloth—anything that has strong associations for you with the love of God, and thus has become a sacramental object of us, through which we feel the healing current of the presence of the Healer.

Another suggestion is to choose some aspect of this miraculous creation to study and to reflect upon: some part of the human body, perhaps, such as the eye, the brain, the hands, or one of the vital organs. Or really study, or think about the structure of a tree, a plant, a mountain, a molecule, the atomic structure, a star. . . .

If you are feeling a loss of the awareness of God's presence, one of the most helpful things to do is to learn about the lives of some of the great lovers of God through history. Or learn about someone who has been transformed by God in this present time. The person need not be a great saint or mystic. He or she could be some ordinary person (are there any *ordinary* persons?) whom you know, one who has experienced God and whose life has been changed through that encounter. . . .

What sacramental experience of God comes to you through human relationships? Think now of the persons in your life whose love has comforted, empowered, nurtured you, believed in you, been there for you when you most needed it. Think of those who have helped you reach for your deepest self, whose love releases and does not constrict, who not only have compassion for your weaknesses and hurt, but who also *delight* in you.

Think about one special person whose love is there for you. Think about this person. Reflect and meditate on this person. Here again is God's presence. The way this person feels about you and responds to you, and reaches out to you is not only a miraculous reality in itself, but is also a hint, a taste of the way God feels about you—a million times more!

Now think about the persons *you* love most in the world. You long for their fulfillment and happiness. When they hurt, you hurt with them. When they are happy you feel their joy at the very core of your heart. Sharing their burdens and problems does not feel like sacrifice, even when it is painful. You would rather be there sharing the pain with them than be off enjoying yourself with someone you love less. (I am speaking now of the persons you *really* love, not the ones you think you *ought* to love.) You are aware of their faults and weaknesses, but it has not the slightest effect on your love. No matter what they did, you would never abandon them. You also know that you cannot constrain or force their response. You would rather not have their response at all if it came forced out of obedience or duty or guilt. You want their love to be free and spontaneous, because they delight in you, as you do in them.

Meditate on your feeling about these persons for a while. Here is God's presence. The way you feel is a tiny taste, a faint shadow of how God feels about you and each one of us. We are made in God's image, the scriptures tell us. Therefore, we are able to taste, experience, manifest a slight measure of what God feels in an unlimited way about every particle of creation.

Think of an occasion when you felt a passionate longing to heal, to help, to comfort, to support. It may be linked with fiery indignation over injustice, greed, communal indifference, insensitivity towards the homeless, abuse of children and the elderly, neglect of the ill, abuse of the body of this earth (its soil, forests, water, atmosphere). You felt an energy flooding through you like a powerful river to involve yourself, to reach out, to become part of the transformation. Here is God's presence sorrowing, grieving, flaming, fighting through you! Here is God's impassioned heart, speaking directly to your heart. Here again, is the sacramental presence to be found, pulling you into the core of that love which hurts with every part of the hurting world.

Join with others, either with a committed group or one or two persons who are searching for a deepened experience of and encounter with God in their lives. Especially join with those who have already had some depth experiences of God's love. Be where they are. Talk to some of them and ask their help and prayers. Meet with them for prayer and sharing, on a regular basis if possible. The living experience of God is contagious!

Finally, choose one of the Gospels to read or reread. You might want to choose the Gospel of Luke which focuses with so much power on Jesus as the Healer. I have heard the fifteenth chapter of Luke called "the Gospel within the Gospels." If the rest of the Bible were lost, and we had only that one chapter, it would show us directly into the center of God's heart.

Read the Gospel you choose as if you had never read it, or even heard of it before. As you read, pay special attention to what Jesus says, and above all, to what he *does*. Reflect on the nature of God who is shown through this person. God is *like* the person. . . .

Perhaps the most important thing of all to remember is that all of these actions, exercises, reflections, are rooted in God's grace. We are not seeking a reluctant God who is hiding. Our very longing to feel closer to God exists because God already loves us, longs for us, has reached us, and spoken to us.

We love, because he first loved us.

—John 4:19, NRSV

Therefore, we can explore, experiment, try the new frontiers with expectant joy and confidence because, in fact, we are responding to the presence which has already and forever found us, the heart that holds us.

—Flora Slosson Wuellner
Heart of Healing, Heart of Light

— FEASTING AT THE TABLE OF DAILY LIFE —

Today, my God, I am asking you to bring back my heart from wherever it has wandered. My enthusiasm has waned. I feel like a dried-up brook. I reach for the hem of your garment. I can't find it. Yet even in this darkness you have prepared a feast. The feast is one of remembering the days of old when my brook was gushing with life. The feast is a reminder that there will always be a bit of solid ground to stand on or wings to fly with. The feast is a wonderful quote that I found in my mailbox today, exactly the tonic to help me celebrate the darkness. This anonymous quote, found in the home of David Larson, M.D., says:

> When we walk to the edge of all the light we have and take that step into the darkness of the unknown, we must believe that one of two things will happen . . . There will be something solid for us to stand on, or we will be taught to fly.

Ah! What a song for my straying heart! Yes, the beautiful thing about this darkness is that it has not prevented me from coming to the table of daily life with wide-open eyes. If it is darkness I must eat, I will eat it with reverence. For I know that in the middle of this darkness I will be given solid ground or wings.

Yet as I pray to you these days, I miss my heart. Do you know where it is? Have you seen it, my God? My poet's heart has dried up. It is gone. There is nothing left. That part of me that could see in the dark is gone. That part of me that could still feel when all the world had turned to ashes is gone.

So what is left on this barren spring day? What is left of the poet's heart? A tiny ray of hope that comes from remembering! That's all that's left, but it's enough to begin the feast.

I remember the days when I held the hands of those who were stumbling, always able to show them another path or point out another star. I remember being able to pick up another's heart and hold it during the dry seasons. But today I can't find enough of my own heart to pick up the heart of another. The poet in me has gone to some sad brook where the waters are dried up. The only ray of hope left is that the brook still remembers that the waters have been there. The parched ground remembers as it looks to the heavens. It is waiting as all lovers must wait. The parched ground is my heart and it, too, remembers that the waters have been there. Never say that all is lost. It is remembering that blesses and saves us. My poet's heart may be gone today, but I have enough vision left. I have enough memory left to feast for a long, long time. And if things get really bad on this once-solid ground, I think I could learn to fly. . . .

O elusive God! Why have you gone away? Is it because I want to be in control of this search?

I do not understand this fruitless search. I feel like a bloodhound on your trail. The scent of you is so near. But when I get you treed, there are no hunters around to help me. I cannot reach you alone. I cannot shoot you from the skies. You refuse to come down. Then just when I think I've found you, you become a nomad again. You are so like your friend Abraham, always on the move, a nomadic, wandering God. You are an ever-moving, always-hiding God.

Or is it otherwise? Am I the one who is moving? Are you the hunter who remains quiet, waiting for the beloved to surrender? O God, throw me a crumb of quiet to soothe my restless, wandering heart. I am tired of seeking you. I know that I'll find you on the day I allow myself to be found by you. But I am not that tame yet. . . .

The Harvest of God: Feasting on Your Theophanies

It was only a small wind
    rather gentle, like a breeze.
It blew a strand of hair across my forehead
    and I knew that it was God.

I was awakened by a tiny gleam of light
    it slipped through my curtain, onto my face.
It drew me to my feet and on to the window
    Drawing back the curtains
dawn stepped softly into my room.
    I knew that it was God.

In the middle of my loneliness
    the phone rang.
A voice I knew so well, said
    "Hello, I love you."
Love stirred in my soul
    I knew that it was God.

Rain fell gently on the thirsty ground.
    Slowly, carefully, steadily it came
to an earth parched with waiting.
    Through those holy raindrops
I walked, unafraid—without an umbrella.
    I knew that it was God.

It was only a little bitterness I thought
    but it wouldn't leave my heart.

It hung around my soul for ages
    until a storm came, violent and terrifying.
It shook me to the depths of my being
    and blew all the bitterness away.
I knew that it was God.

It was only a Silver Maple
    but in the morning's sunlight
It was filled with heaven.
    I stood in a trance
as one touched by angel wings.
    I knew that it was God.

O God, I cried,
    Endearing One, I love you!
You cannot hide from me.
    Between the cracks of daily life
I find you waiting
    to be adored.
You slip into my life
    like night and day
    like stars and sunshine.
I know that you are God.

        —Macrina Wiederkehr
        A Tree Full of Angels

— PRAYER OF THE FORSAKEN —

Every faith journey is tailor-made. Our sense of God's absence does not come to us in any preset timetable. We cannot simply draw some universal road map that everyone will be able to follow. . . .

Since there is no special sequence in the life of prayer, we simply do not move from one stage to the next knowing, for example, that at stages five and twelve we will experience abandonment by God. It would be easier that way, but then we would be describing a mechanical arrangement rather than a living relationship.

A Living Relationship
That is the next thing that should be said about our sense of the absence of God, namely, that we are entering into a living relationship that begins and develops in mutual freedom. God grants us perfect free-

dom because he desires creatures who freely choose to be in relationship with him. Through the Prayer of the Forsaken, we are learning to give to God the same freedom. Relationships of this kind can never be manipulated or forced.

If we could make the Creator of heaven and earth appear at our beck and call, we would not be in communion with the God of Abraham, Isaac, and Jacob. We do that with objects or idols. But God, the great iconoclast, is constantly smashing our false images of who he is and what he is like.

Can you see how our very sense of the absence of God is, therefore, an unsuspected grace? In the very act of hiddenness, God is slowly weaning us of fashioning him in our own image. Like Aslan, the Christ figure in *The Chronicles of Narnia*, God is wild and free and comes at will. By refusing to be a puppet on our string or a genie in our bottle, God frees us from our false, idolatrous images. . . .

It is not that we disbelieve in God, but more profoundly, we wonder what kind of God we believe in. Is God good and intent upon our goodness, or is God cruel, sadistic, and a tyrant?

We discover that the workings of faith, hope, and love become themselves subject to doubt. Our personal motivations become suspect. We worry whether this act or that thought is inspired by fear, vanity, and arrogance rather than faith, hope, and love.

Like a frightened child, we walk cautiously through the dark mists that now surround the Holy of Holies. We become tentative and unsure of ourselves. Nagging questions assail us with a force they never had before. "Is prayer only a psychological trick?" "Does evil ultimately win out?" "Is there any real meaning in the universe?" "Does God really love me?"

Through all of this, paradoxically, God is purifying our faith by threatening to destroy it. We are led to a profound and holy distrust of all superficial drives and human strivings. We know more deeply than ever before our capacity for self-deception. . . .

The Prayer of Complaint

Is there any kind of prayer we can engage in when we feel forsaken? Yes—we can begin by praying the Prayer of Complaint. . . .

The best way I know to relearn this time-honored approach to God is by praying that part of the Psalter traditionally known as the "Lament Psalms." The ancient singers really knew how to complain and their words of anguish and frustration can guide our lips into the prayer we dare not pray alone. They expressed reverence *and* disappointment. "God, whom I praise, break your silence." (Ps. 109:1, JB).

They experienced dogged hope *and* mounting despair. "I am here, calling for your help, praying to you every morning: why do you reject me? Why do you hide your face from me?" (Ps. 88:13-14, JB). They had confidence in the character of God *and* the exasperation at the inaction of God: "I say to God, my rock, 'Why have you forgotten me?' " (Ps. 42:9, NIV).

The Lament Psalms teach us to pray our inner conflicts and contradictions. They allow us to shout out our forsakenness in the dark caverns of abandonment and then hear the echo return to us over and over again. They give us permission to shake our fist at God one moment and break into doxology the next.

—Richard J. Foster
Prayer

— THE VALUE OF DARKNESS —

The way of faith, John of the Cross insists, is necessarily obscure. We drive by night, only seeing a little of the way ahead. We make progress precisely by not understanding, by darkness. In Soho I was coming to see how important this truth is in pastoral work and in political struggle. We need to act on the basis of faith, on an insight that is nourished by darkness, a conviction that has its roots in silence, a vision that is not clear but is firmly based in that mysterious reality which is the darkness of God. If social and political action is not to decay into fanaticism, it needs those deep roots.

For John of the Cross, the dark night is not a negative and destructive experience: it is the experience of fire and light, of the living flame of the love of God, as experienced by finite beings. Faith blinds and dazzles the intellect; the sheer intensity of faith overwhelms it. And the darkness grows always deeper. For the dark night is not a phase, it is a symbol by which John speaks of the whole of reality. All our life and all our activity takes place in the context of this darkness.

The night comes upon us. We are never prepared for it, for the essence of the night is the sense of being out of control, of being bound and controlled by the mysterious working of the Spirit of God. Only later do we identify what has been going on and are able to express it. I believe that the effectiveness of our work for justice in the world is directly related to our encounter with this central core of darkness. For truthful and just action can grow only out of deep roots in truth and justice.

—Kenneth Leech
The Eye of the Storm

WHEN ALL I HEAR IS SILENCE

As the mother understands the wordless child,
the wise teacher hears the stammering boy,
the sage hears the awe-silenced pilgrim,
hear us, our Father, as we hold up to thee
our longings and our need.
In Christ's name. *Amen.*

—Edward Tyler
Prayers in Celebration of the Turning Year

RETREAT  PATTERN

Prayer for Guidance

Faithful Savior, who became one of us to make your way and your Self known to humankind, reveal your way and your Presence to me during these hours of retreat. Help me to lay aside the burdens and concerns of my life and ministry long enough to hear your voice. Lead me into the light of your truth and prepare me for faithful and joyful discipleship. *Amen.*

Silent Listening

Scripture Reading

Luke 4:1-30; Romans 12:1-21; 1 Corinthians 9:1-27; Ephesians 1:1-23
Reflect on each of the passages until they begin to address you and your ministry. Where does each passage bring comfort? Disturb? List any specific actions the passages urge you to take.

Spiritual Reading

Reflection

Mealtime, Rest, Recreation

Journaling

Prayer

Further Spiritual Reading, Reflection, Journaling, Prayer

Eucharist

Response: Thanksgiving, Offerings, Covenant

Returning to the World

You may use suggestions from the appendix or design your own plan of faithful living, including daily and weekly actions designed to nurture and sustain your life and ministry.

Closing Prayer

Sustaining God, in whom we find our identity and our life, thank you for this time apart with you. I offer to you all of my life that I am able to give. Accept and make holy the gift of self I bring and send me from this place renewed, refreshed, and redirected for effective ministry in your name. *Amen.*

2.
WHEN OTHERS TELL ME WHO I AM

The towering truth of Dietrich Bonhoeffer's personal and very poetic reflection on his identity is found in the final lines of his poem, "Who Am I?": "Whoever I am, Thou knowest, O God, I am thine!" Deeply committed, deeply spiritual, fully engaged with the world, and a prisoner for his convictions, he shares the conflicts and questions openly and without embarrassment. And yet, the bottom line is clear. His life is given to and secure in the hands of God.

The context of Bonhoeffer's poem is far different from the context of our ministry, and yet there are similar questions and conflicts that confront every clergyperson in the course of a life of ministry. That is, the environment is always pressing in on the identity of the clergyperson. A part of that pressing comes from those who wish to shape the pastor's identity, another part of that pressing comes from the cultural setting, and still another from the religious traditions in which the pastor labors.

A congregation, an agency, and the institutional church itself are always in the process of giving definition to their leadership. Pastors cannot escape the sometimes gentle and sometimes nearly brutal attempts to define not only the pastor's role but the pastor's identity. How is the pastor to continue the process of self-discovery in the midst of pastoral ministry? By offering all of one's life, ministry, and future to God who is made known to us in Jesus Christ.

If you are preparing for ministry, the following illustrations will help you to recognize several of the ways in which others seek to tell you who you are. If you are already active in ministry, you may well multiply this list with illustrations of your own. The first illustration comes from my first appointment after seminary. The second is from a later appointment. And the third is from the experience of a clergy couple.

Our modest (in amount, value, and quality) belongings were on the lawn of the parsonage while the furniture of the former pastor was being loaded into the waiting van. As my wife and I drove up, we noticed three elderly men seated on our davenport about ten feet away from the front door of the parsonage. This was to be our home and our parish, so thinking I would make my first pastoral call, I approached the three gentlemen, introduced myself as the new pastor, and began to engage them in conversation. One of the three asked me if I could speak German. Since this was an area where many German immigrants had settled and the German language was still common, I used my best college German and responded in the language they loved, "Of course." The next question, now in the German language, was, "Can you preach in German?" My response, also in German, had to be no. Before I could explain how hard I would try to meet their personal needs, they responded in German, almost in unison, "Then you can never become a pastor."

I did become their pastor. We learned to love each other and I had the memorial service for two of these saints before I left the community. And yet, their expectations for my pastoral ministry and leadership among them were never fully realized. They never stopped their efforts nor lost their desire to shape not only my ministry, but my identity as a Christian. Their intentions did not grow out of some evil design, but it was a natural consequence of their understanding and hopes for pastoral leadership. Nevertheless, the pressure to conform was great.

The moving van had not yet pulled away from the parsonage of a later appointment, when two members of the congregation came to the door and, on our invitation, entered to tell us how glad they were to see us, leave food for our evening meal, and give subtle hints about directions they expected their new pastor to follow. Before the week was out, a sizable number of persons had stopped by at the office or the parsonage to share directions with this new pastor. Some were subtle and some were explicit, but the intent was clear—the shaping of a pastor to meet the expectations of a congregation. Many of the expectations were noble, some were clearly outside the scope of Christian charity, many were just plain silly. Frequently I was challenged by 1 Corinthians 9. How could I become all things to all people without losing my own soul? Only by finding my identity in God. An identity being shaped and transformed by the Spirit in the context of daily pastoral ministry lived out of a disciplined life of prayer and reflection.

A young clergy couple came to their bishop perplexed by the pressures to compromise their understanding of who they were and what their respective roles were to be in the community and the congregations under their care. Like every other pastor, all aspects of their lives were under scrutiny and they received persistent pressures to adopt styles and methods of parenting, community involvement, male and female roles, and pastoral leadership that would reflect the desires of their many evaluators. Some of the suggestions came from pure intentions, most from highly motivated persons, and all with the goal of defining the persons and leadership of their pastors. With an intervention by an outside consultant, support for the pastors and congregations by denominational leadership, a disciplined process of assessment and prayer, these congregations and their pastors grew in the strength of their own identity, in their relationship to God in Christ, and in faithful ministry to their communities and the world.

These three illustrations reflect some of the voices that seek to tell pastors who they are. Stop now and think of your own experience. Who is trying to tell you who you are? Someone in the congregation? In your denominational structure? Perhaps, even in your extended family? This pressure is not new. Read again verses sixteen to thirty of the fourth chapter of the Gospel of Luke and note not only the visionary sermon, but the congregational response. Peter and John on the way to prayer (Acts 3), Stephen refusing to be defined by the traditions of the synagogue (Acts 6 and 7), and Peter's vision at Joppa that shattered the image he had of himself and of others (Acts 10), indicate that the earliest Christian leaders not only faced pressures that sought to define who they were, but they found strength in God to live out their true identity and call. Their relationship to God was the defining factor in their lives.

Every pastor who has a measure of self-awareness will recognize the subtle and not so subtle efforts to define the ministry and the person involved in ministry. Pastors who seek to follow and obey no other voice than the voice of God in Jesus Christ will discover that this model of ministry is not always the one desired by congregations and almost never by culture. Congregations may say they want spiritual leaders, but when they see a pastor disciplined in the spiritual life, vulnerable, caring for others, focused on God and God's reign, they are often uneasy and in a variety of ways, try to shape that pastor's identity and ministry into a more tame and tempered model. Radical faith makes many uncomfortable, and since it is not easy to dismiss, there are often more direct attempts to dull its passion and silence its voice. The world is indeed seeking to press us into its own mold (Rom. 12:2) and the only way to avoid that cultural shaping is to stand daily in·the transforming grace of God (Rom. 12:1-21).

At the center of our faith is the belief that we are not identified by our ancestors, our degrees, our pastoral appointments, or by the views of others. Our identity is found in the creator God who made us and in Jesus Christ who redeems us, transforms, sustains, and sends us to live faithful lives in the world that God loves (Eph. 1:1-23).

Clarity about who we are is found in God and in intimate companionship with God. This intimate companionship does not occur accidentally. It is the result of our consistent response to God's persistent invitation to relationship. And it is in this daily and intimate companionship that our identity as persons and as pastors becomes clear.

The pressures to conform, to turn aside from our true identity, come not only from congregations and institutions. There are those inner needs that clamor for attention and lead us to seek and even create identity that is not founded in God. Even the pressure to conform can remind us who we are and to whom we belong. The Christian minister knows only one Savior and only one Lord. When this awareness begins to settle over us, the pressures to conform lose their painful sting and their seductive power.

A colleague of mine was called to lead a congregational meeting on his birthday. His elementary-school-age sons presented him with a pair of Superman shorts for his birthday and asked that he wear them to the evening meeting. He did. The meeting was controversial and, try as he did to remain objective, there was pressure to choose sides. When he did not choose sides, anger was directed at him and he was feeling overwhelmed and depressed by the hostility he was experiencing. Then he remembered his Superman shorts and the love of his family. He thought to himself, my sons and my wife love me and this momentary pain is insignificant compared to the warmth of their love. In the midst of the meeting he reflected on his baptism and God's love and how he found meaning and life in that love. He then began to see how foolish were his fears, anxiety, and growing anger at those whose behavior was so immature. On the drive home he reflected on how easily he had forgotten who he was and how quickly he had been drawn into acting like someone he did not want to be. It was an important learning.

Where is our identity to be found? The answer is as old as the *Heidelberg Catechism:* "In the truth that I belong—body and soul, in life and in death—not to myself but to my faithful Savior, Jesus Christ." You will face a lifetime of subtle and overt efforts to define your ministry and yourself. Remembering to whom you belong gives direction as you fashion your life and ministry under the guidance of the One who has called you to this time and place of ministry.

SPIRITUAL  READINGS

— WHO AM I? —

Who am I? They often tell me
I stepped from my cell's confinement
calmly, cheerfully, firmly,
like a Squire from his country-house.

Who am I? They often tell me
I used to speak to my warders
freely and friendly and clearly,
as though it were mine to command.

Who am I? They also tell me
I would bear the days of misfortune
equably, smilingly, proudly,
like one accustomed to win.

Am I then really that which other men tell of?
Or am I only what I myself know of myself,
restless and longing and sick, like a bird in a cage,
struggling for breath, as though hands were compressing my throat,
yearning for colours, for flowers, for the voices of birds,
thirsting for words of kindness, for neighbourliness,
trembling with anger at despotisms and petty humiliation,
tossing in expectation of great events,
powerlessly trembling for friends at an infinite distance,
weary and empty at praying, at thinking, at making,
faint, and ready to say farewell to it all.

Who am I? This or the other?
Am I one person today and tomorrow another?
Am I both at once? A hypocrite before others,
and before myself a contemptibly woebegone weakling?
Or is something within me still like a beaten army
fleeing in disorder from victory already achieved?

Who am I? They mock me, these lonely questions of mine.
Whoever I am, thou knowest, O God, I am thine!

—Dietrich Bonhoeffer
Letters and Papers from Prison

45

— TAKE HEED —

Let us consider, What it is to take heed to ourselves.

See that the work of saving grace be thoroughly wrought in your own souls. Take heed to yourselves, lest you be void of that saving grace of God which you offer to others, and be strangers to the effectual working of that gospel which you preach; and lest, while you proclaim to the world the necessity of a Saviour, your own hearts should neglect him, and you should miss of an interest in him and his saving benefits. Take heed to yourselves, lest you perish, while you call upon others to take heed of perishing; and lest you famish yourselves while you prepare food for them. . . .

Take heed to yourselves, lest your example contradict your doctrine, and lest you lay such stumbling-blocks before the blind, as may be the occasion of their ruin; lest you unsay with your lives, what you say with your tongues; and be the greatest hinderers of the success of your own labours.

—Richard Baxter
The Reformed Pastor

— THE COMPULSIVE MINISTER —

Thomas Merton writes in the introduction to his *The Wisdom of the Desert:*

> Society . . . was regarded [by the Desert Fathers] as a shipwreck from which each single individual man had to swim for his life . . . These were men who believed that to let oneself drift along, passively accepting the tenets and values of what they knew as society, was purely and simply a disaster.

This observation leads us straight to the core of the problem. Our society is not a community radiant with the love of Christ, but a dangerous network of domination and manipulation in which we can easily get entangled and lose our soul. The basic question is whether we ministers of Jesus Christ have not already been so deeply molded by the seductive powers of our dark world that we have become blind to our own and other people's fatal state and have lost the power and motivation to swim for our lives.

Just look for a moment at our daily routine. In general we are very busy people. We have many meetings to attend, many visits to make, many services to lead. Our calendars are filled with appointments, our days and weeks filled with engagements, and our years filled with plans and projects. There is seldom a period in which we do not know what to do, and we move through life in such a distracted way that we do not even take the time and rest to wonder if any of the things we think, say, or do are *worth* thinking, saying, or doing. We simply go along with the many "musts" and "oughts" that have been handed on to us, and we live with them as if they were authentic translations of the Gospel of our Lord. People must be motivated to come to church, youth must be entertained, money must be raised, and above all everyone must be happy. Moreover, we ought to be on good terms with the church and civil authorities; we ought to be liked or at least respected by a fair majority of our parishioners; we ought to move up in the ranks according to schedule; and we ought to have enough vacation and salary to live a comfortable life. Thus we are busy people just like all other busy people, rewarded with the rewards which are rewarded to busy people!

All this is simply to suggest how horrendously secular our ministerial lives tend to be. Why is this so? Why do we children of the light so easily become conspirators with the darkness? The answer is quite simple. Our identity, our sense of self, is at stake. Secularity is a way of being dependent on the responses of our milieu. The secular or false self is the self which is fabricated, as Thomas Merton says, by social compulsions. "Compulsive" is indeed the best adjective for the false self. It points to the need for ongoing and increasing affirmation. Who am I? I am the one who is liked, praised, admired, disliked, hated or despised. Whether I am a pianist, a businessman or a minister, what matters is how I am perceived by my world. If being busy is a good thing, then I must be busy. If having money is a sign of real freedom, then I must claim my money. If knowing many people proves my importance, I will have to make the necessary contacts. The compulsion manifests itself in the lurking fear of failing and the steady urge to prevent this by gathering more of the same—more work, more money, more friends.

These very compulsions are at the basis of the two main enemies of the spiritual life: anger and greed. They are the inner side of a secular life, the sour fruits of our worldly dependencies. What else is anger than the impulsive response to the experience of being deprived? When my sense of self depends on what others say of me, anger is a quite natural reaction to a critical word. And when my sense of self depends on what I can acquire, greed flares up when my desires are frustrated. Thus greed and anger are the brother and sister of a false self fabricated by the social compulsion of an unredeemed world.

Anger in particular seems close to a professional vice in the contemporary ministry. Pastors are angry at their leaders for not leading and at their followers for not following. They are angry at those who do not come to church for not coming and angry at those who do come for coming without enthusiasm. They are angry at their families, who make them feel guilty, and angry at themselves for not being who they want to be. This is not an open, blatant, roaring anger, but an anger hidden behind the smooth word, the smiling face, and the polite handshake. It is a frozen anger, an anger which settles into a biting resentment and slowly paralyzes a generous heart. If there is anything that makes the ministry look grim and dull, it is this dark, insidious anger in the servants of Christ.

It is not so strange that Anthony and his fellow monks considered it a spiritual disaster to accept passively the tenets and values of their society. They had come to appreciate how hard it is not only for the individual Christian but also for the church itself to escape the seductive compulsions of the world. What was their response? They escaped from the sinking ship and swam for their lives. And the place of salvation is called desert, the place of solitude.

—Henri J. M. Nouwen
The Way of the Heart

— SELF-EXAMINATION —

Socrates said, "The unexamined life is not worth living." To look after and care for the soul, according to Socrates, was more important than money, honor, and even reputation. The first duty was "to know thyself. . . . For once we *know* ourselves, we may then learn how to *care for* ourselves, but otherwise we never shall." Even the fantasy character Alice in Wonderland asks the question, "Who *in the world* am I? Ah, that's the great puzzle!"

One of the greatest dangers stalking all religious leaders is that of becoming so busy or so bored, so proud or so depressed; that the things they desire most, as well as their actions, go unexamined. Because we want it so much, we assume it is right for us and that we are therefore doing it well.

An essential practice for being an effective leader is, therefore, that one must continually examine one's own life. First, examine the character and structure of one's life when out of the public eye: Who am I? What thoughts do I entertain? To what private and secret activities do I give myself? Second, examine the quality and character of one's life and work when one is in the public eye: What are my values and behaviors as a leader? To what do I give myself? What are the true results of my leadership?

Without exception the Reformers sounded the call and set the example of self-examination. Martin Luther taught that the last activity of each day should be to examine one's motives and actions of the day, and then give the day to God and go to sleep, that while we are out of the way in the hours of this momentary death, God may finish our work, doing for us as we sleep what we could not accomplish in our wakeful hours.

Calvin tellingly describes the need when he says that "without knowledge of self there is no knowledge of God . . . [and] without knowledge of God there is no knowledge of self." John Wesley modeled self-examination as a continuing essential for the religious leader. In his early years he set aside time in every day for the "examination." Later, he began the practice of setting aside each Saturday for self-examination. Finally, in his later years, he developed the habit and inner clock to pause for the first five minutes of each hour to examine the hour past.

Problems enough are evident in congregations whose pastors are confused over their roles as a leader. There are more and deeper problems when a pastor forgets he or she is a person. The study and practice of leadership begins with our interior life—it is our own identity and self-understanding that influences all other leadership behaviors and relationships.

Congregations expect competent church leaders, but they also want pastors who possess inner character and integrity—a congruency between what they profess and what they do. For a variety of reasons, the journey inward is resisted by many. Some are afraid, others are too busy or feel guilty for taking the time, as the urgent demands and problems press in on them.

The interior life of the leader does indeed work its way out in all other aspects of ministry. The Christian leader [according to Thomas Oden] "must not be a slave to one's own unexamined passions. Otherwise the souls entrusted to one's care may be subject to manipulation by the supposed career, whose passions are projected on to the relationship." These foundation blocks of Christian leadership—to grow into childlikeness, to journey toward being poor in spirit, to desire leadership in order to serve, and to continually examine one's private and public life—form the vortex of effective ministry. They are not barriers to leadership; they are doorways to freedom. They are not to be enjoined with gloom and doom, but with spontaneity and joy. The possibility of each is given to us as a promise from God.

—Norman Shawchuck and Roger Heuser
Leading the Congregation

49

— SERVANT PASTOR —

As I announced to a student that I practice my ministry as a "servant," I heard myself defining my servant role. I am a servant of the servants of God, who are the laity, in Celia Allison Hahn's words in *Lay Voices in an Open Church*, "the Open Church, the Church in the World." When all expressions of ministry originate in Christ, the Servant, identified in the Servant Poems in the book of Isaiah and pictured in that table scene in the Gospel of John, the offices and titles of ministry cease being signs of status, and the tension between clergy and laity is eliminated. Each and all are servants, with service defined by the work each does. "Servant" is the word traced back to Christ, who inspires and legitimates all forms of Christian service. "Servant," is the title that spares the young woman the need to say, "I can't be above a guy!" "Servant" is the word that should answer the angry laywoman's protest and the clergywomen's commitment to turning ecclesiastical hierarchies on their sides, from plastic cones to straws!

It all happens through Christ's words, "I have set an example for you." Christ is a Christian's model for ministry. When a student prompted me to express that definition, I felt the thrill of learning (like Albert Schweitzer's unforeseen, unsought phrase) "reverence for life." I had been introduced to the joy of a word for laity and clergy in the community called "Christian." Christ, modeling the word servant, imparts a reverence to every Christian's ministry.

The happiness of that practice of ministry is also the joy of finding a title that is inclusive. The word servant not only lacks status, but is also free of bias or gender preference. Servants have no occasions to quibble over pronouns! I find that to be an exciting alternative to all the traditional terms for clergy that, just by being named, conjure exclusively male images of the ordained ministry. I am also excited about the word's elimination of any order of clergy over laity. "Servant" is the word that holds the potential of introducing ordained and unordained to each other. I feel the thrill of pursuing that introduction with laity as well as with my clergy sisters and brothers. The thrill is the exploration of our common ministry and all we'll learn as we let the word servant teach us who we are. . . .

My stole is a towel! I had just assimilated one more lesson taught by another clergywoman ministering to me through words about her "fabric of faith." My stole is a towel! I find that thought to be just as exciting as the word servant. And just as challenging! For how many years have clergymen (and the gender is intentional) put on the stole, the sign of their office, never identifying it as a towel, a sign of service? Now clergywomen, for whom a towel worn as an apron has been their traditional garment for "women's work," can model a stole's full meaning: a pastor's towel!

"Stole" is a strip of cloth that makes the pastoral office inclusive, for it is the towel of service designed to be worn by clergymen and clergy-women. "Servant" is the word that makes all offices and expressions of ministry an unranked service, for it is the title intended for every baptized Christian. These are lessons waiting to be taught by women and men whose classroom is a congregation and whose life is the curriculum. My prayer for my ministry is that I may be a servant (pastor) of the servants of God (laity), equipping them for their ministry in the world.

—Martha B. Kriebel
A Stole Is a Towel

— FRUITS OF CONTEMPLATION —

I would not accept the monk in his cell or the theologian in his study as *spiritual* unless the fruit of their effort is such that it finds its way to nourish the servant motive in those who do the work of the world. This, it seems to me, is one of the major reasons why that mediating institution, the church, is so important: to help the fruits of contemplation and theological reflection become an animating force that sustains legions of persons as *servants* as they wield their influence on governments, businesses, schools, hospitals, families, communities, and in the church itself. Thus I see churches as (potentially) formative institutions that nurture spirituality in those they reach *and,* in so doing, nurture themselves so as to sustain themselves as models that encourage other institutions to be optimally serving to (and therefore caring for) all persons whose lives they influence. The two roles, nurture of spirituality in individuals and model for others as a serving institution, are closely linked. In my view, *any institution that carries these two roles effectively is a church*—regardless of its theological position.

—Robert K. Greenleaf
Spirituality as Leadership

— EMBRACING ORDINARINESS —

True ordinariness is tangible holiness. We can sense this particularly when we are with persons who have the courage and trust in God to "simply be themselves."

Jim Fenhagen, the Dean of General Theological Seminary, relates the story of a seminarian who was sitting near him during an address by

Archbishop Desmond Tutu. After the talk was over, the student turned to Dean Fenhagen and said: "Today I met a holy man." When he asked the student to elaborate, he replied that in Tutu's presence he was able to experience Christ in his own life.

I think all of us have experienced this with certain people. I remember visiting someone who was so real, undefensive, accepting, and self-aware that during the visit I felt no stress or anxiety at all. I could be myself; it was enough. I even had the strange sensation after I left him that I had not aged while in his presence! After all, how could I? There was no pressure when I was with him. . . .

Due to our lack of complete trust in God's revelation that we are made in the divine image and likeness, most of us get caught up in trying to be extra-ordinary. We become insecure and are tempted to rest our sense of self on something less than God's love for us. As a result, we waste our energy worrying about whether we are liked, respected, effective, or as good as other people.

We certainly can learn from Jesus' example in this regard. In contrast to our concern with what other people think of us Jesus did not compare himself to others. We cannot find a single instance in the New Testament where he clung to his divinity. He wasn't obsessed with his image as we so often are with ours. Instead, he was only concerned with: 1) trying to be who he was called to be (obedience); 2) being in solidarity with others (community); 3) doing everything in the right Spirit (love). This is only possible for us when we, like Jesus, 1) feel deeply loved by God; 2) see the essential value and challenge of "simply" being ourselves (ordinary); 3) resist the temptation to create a false image of ourselves. Both our anxieties and the values of our society can seduce us into trying to develop, or hold onto, another image of self—even if it be a seemingly desirable or good one.

The Spirit of ordinariness invites each of us to follow the will of God by trying to find out what our inner motivations and talents are and then to express them without reserve or self-consciousness. This is true ordinariness. Although the call to be ordinary may be simple, it is not easy! And, because very few of us appreciate this subtle, yet profound, distinction, "being ordinary" is an extraordinary event in our times. . . .

As is the case with the call to simply be ourselves, listening to God through our own deep experiences of self is a basic lesson of spiritual discernment. Yet most of us don't do this. Instead, we often answer the secular calls to be successful, unique, secure, perfect, or right. We try to accomplish another goal which we believe will protect us from facing our dependence on God or keep us from experiencing life as a mystery we can't fathom or control. Maybe that is why one of the most essential

52

challenges we face is to truly accept our limits. When we do this, the opportunity for personal growth and development is almost limitless. And, as we might expect, accepting our limits is not very popular. In fact, it is countercultural.

—Robert J. Wicks
Touching the Holy

— HE WAS ALIVE AND HE WAS REAL —

Reverend Hoff was a young man around my parents' age, full of kinetic energy. I have no real memory of his appearance. Because I loved him, he has become tall and handsome in my mind, but that is neither here nor there. He loved me back, which was his chief beauty.

A bachelor with no children of his own, he was remarkably good with those of us who gazed up at him from belt level. I know now it was my parents' friendship he was after, but he never condescended to me. When we spoke I had his full attention, so that his first gift to me was his assurance that I was a whole human being, young as I was, and worthy of his regard. . . .

Most of my memories come from around our supper table. Reverend Hoff, catching an airborne fly with one hand. Reverend Hoff, laughing with his head thrown back. Reverend Hoff, so caught up in heated conversation that he let his meat loaf get cold. He was alive, he was real, and I was too young to know that ministers came any other way. So his second gift to me was my early belief that to be God's person you had to be vital and genuine. Later on, when I ran into the minty-breathed, smooth-talking, thin-lipped variety of preacher, I did not even blink. I knew they were counterfeits.

I recall one dinner table conversation in particular. After several months of visiting the church and getting to know Reverend Hoff, my parents decided to join the congregation. This was no small concession for two people who had sworn off organized religion. My father was an estranged Roman Catholic and my mother a disaffected southern Methodist, but something about this vital, genuine young man made them willing to reopen a door they had both agreed to close.

"We have decided to join your church," my father announced one night over supper, as pleased as if he were declaring peace after a long cold war.

"Please don't," Reverend Hoff said, and it was all I could do to hold on to my fork. "If you join the church, things will change between us. I won't be able to talk to you in the same way anymore, and that would be such a loss for me." So we did not join, not officially, but the relationship deepened all the same. When my mother's mother died, my father was out of town and Reverend Hoff was the first person at the door. Officially or not, he was our pastor and we were his, which constituted a third gift: an experience of mutual ministry that transcended our prescribed roles.

One reason Reverend Hoff needed us to talk to was that things were not going well at the church. Dublin, Ohio, had once been a quiet country town, but by the time we arrived it was becoming a suburb of Columbus. City folk like us were seen as intruders, whom the country folk treated much like their yard dogs treated strangers. They bristled and growled as urban aliens challenged their politics, their economics and their moral values. I once believed that the issue was civil rights, but I think now that was a trick of memory, a transposition from another time. The problem was similar, however. Would the church raise its drawbridge and shrink from the changing world outside, or would its doors remain open to all comers, even if that meant that the world inside the church was bound to change? Reverend Hoff was willing to take the risk, but his congregation was not behind him.

Secret meetings were held. Anonymous letters were written. Driving into the churchyard on Sunday morning was like pulling into a political convention. People stood in small clumps around their cars and spoke in low voices, flicking their eyes this way and that as others approached. If the newcomer was a friend, the circle widened. If he or she was not, the circle dissolved, its members coughing and clearing their throats as they put out their cigarettes and headed for church.

In the midst of this hard time, Reverend Hoff came to supper. Before we sat down to eat, he let me show him my latest project. It was a birdbath full of tadpoles—a kind of frog nursery—which I had devised after discovering some of the neighbor boys stomping tadpoles down by the creek. I could not save them all, but I liked to think that this many, at least, would become frogs. I showed Reverend Hoff how some of them had back legs and some had all four. He dipped his hand into the water and came up under a little half-inch frog that sat on the pad of his finger like a jewel. The frog watched us and we watched the frog, as our chests swelled and fell with the same breath of life.

Then my mother called that supper was ready. It was a long meal that night, the three adults still hunched over the table as my sisters and I drifted off to sleep. Later that week Reverend Hoff called to make sure I would be in church the following Sunday. He wanted me to hear his sermon, he said, so I sat up front and listened to him talk about the beautiful diversity of God's creation.

It is our duty to be awed by it, he said, and then all of a sudden he was telling the congregation about a little girl he knew who kept tadpoles in a birdbath so that she could watch over them, and how her care for those creatures was part of God's care for the whole world. It was a spotlit moment for me, not only to hear myself spoken of in church but also to know that my life was part of God's life, and that something as ordinary as a tadpole connected the two. It was then I first understood the true power of the pulpit—not to deliver holy truth from on high but to connect ordinary people's everyday experience with the extraordinary presence of God. Years and years later, that is still what I am trying to do. I am still preaching tadpole sermons in hopes that a few of them will sprout legs.

By the end of that year, Reverend Hoff was gone. His congregation hanged him in effigy, and he took the hint, packing his bags and walking out the door of the freshly painted parsonage. Although it broke my heart, his departure was his final gift to me. While I have gone on to serve the church myself, I have never gotten it confused with the kingdom, nor have I deluded myself about my own power to change the system. I am a corrupt servant in a corrupt institution, but every now and then God uses one or both of us to redeem a little something, and that little bit turns out to be enough to live on.

—Barbara Brown Taylor
The Preaching Life

— SELF-PORTRAIT —

A story told by Oskar Kokoschka, about his visit to a London museum, can help us reach a better understanding of caring in the context of aging.

> I was in England during World War I, moneyless and miserable. My wife, who is younger and more courageous than I am, said: "Let's go to a museum for relief." There was destruction in the whole world. Not only were bombs being dropped on London—every day we heard of another city being destroyed. Devastation, ruins, the annihilation of a world becoming poorer and sadder. That was bitter. I looked at Rembrandt's last self-portrait; so hideous and broken; so horrible and hopeless; and so wonderfully painted. All at once it came to me: to be able to look at one's fading self in the mirror—see nothing—and paint oneself as the *néant*, the nothingness of man! What a miracle, what an image! In that I found courage and new youth. "Holy Rembrandt," I said. Indeed, I owe my life only to the artists.

There can hardly be a better image of caring than that of the artist who brings new life to people by his honest and fearless self-portrait. Rembrandt painted his sixty-three self-portraits not just as "a model for studies in expression" but as "a search for the spiritual through the channel of his innermost personality." Rembrandt felt that he had to enter into his own self, into his dark cellars as well as into his light rooms, if he really wanted to penetrate the mystery of man's interiority. Rembrandt realized that what is most personal is most universal. While growing in age he was more and more able to touch the core of the human experience, in which individuals in their misery can recognize themselves and find "courage and new youth." We will never be able to really care if we are not willing to paint and repaint constantly our self-portrait, not as a morbid self-preoccupation, but as a service to those who are searching for some light in the midst of the darkness.

—Henri J. M. Nouwen and Walter J. Gaffney
Aging

— I AM A STRANGER HERE ON EARTH —

When God's Word found me for the first time, it made me a stranger on this earth. It placed me in the long succession of the forebears of the faith, who lived as aliens in the promised land (Heb. 11:9). Abraham believed the call which bade him go from his own land into the land of promise; yet, in his old age, after Sarah's death, he received as a "stranger and a sojourner" ground enough for a burial place as his only possession in the promised land (Gen. 23:4). Jacob confessed to Pharaoh that his entire life had been a pilgrimage, briefer and harder still than the pilgrimages of his fathers Isaac and Abraham (Gen. 47:9). When the children of Israel took firm possession of the land of Canaan, they were never allowed to forget that they had been strangers, too, and that they still were. They had been strangers in Egypt (Ex. 22:20), and they remained to that day "strangers and sojourners" in the land which did not belong to them but to God (Lev. 25:23). In a great and festive hour of his life, David included himself with these ancestors, when he said: "For we are strangers before thee and sojourners, as all our fathers were; our days on the earth are like a shadow, and there is no abiding" (I Chron. 29:15).

I am a stranger on earth. Therefore, I confess that I cannot remain here, that my given time is brief. Nor do I have any claim here to houses and possessions. The good things which I enjoy I must thankfully receive, but I must also endure injustice and violence with no one to intercede for me. I have no firm hold on either persons or things. As a stranger, I am subject to the laws of the place where I sojourn. The earth, which nourishes me, has a right to my work and my strength. I have no right to despise the earth on which I live. I owe it loyalty and gratitude. It is my lot to be a stranger and a sojourner, but this cannot become a reason for evading God's call so that I dream away my earthly life with thoughts of heaven.

There is a very godless homesickness for the other world which is not consistent with really finding one's home there. I ought to behave myself like a guest here, with all that entails. I should not stay aloof and refuse to participate in the tasks, joys and sorrows of earth, while I am waiting patiently for the redemption of the divine promise. I am really to wait for the promise and not try to steal it in advance in wishes and dreams. Nothing is said here at all about the homeland itself. I know that it cannot be this earth, and yet I know that the earth is God's and that I am on this earth not only as its guest but as God's wayfarer and sojourner (Ps. 39:14). However, since I am on earth only as a stranger and guest, without rights, without permanent residence, without security, the very God who made me this weak and insignificant has given me one firm pledge for my goal: his Word. This one thing that is certain he will not take away from me; he will keep his Word for me, and in it he will let me sense his power. Where the Word is at home with me, I am able to find my way in the strange land—to find what is right where there is injustice, a place to stand where there is uncertainty, strength for my work, and patience in time of sorrow.

"Do not hide your commandments from me." That is the prayer of the pilgrim in a strange land.

For those who have become strangers on earth, according to God's will and his calling, there is really only one thought that can fill them with dread—that they might no longer recognize God's will, no longer know what God requires of them. Indeed, God is often hidden in the course of our personal lives or in his action in history; but that is not what causes us anguish. No, it is the fear that the revealed commandment of God might be obscured, so that we no longer know from God's Word what we are to do. In the midst of our happy certainty of the commandments of God, this fear overtakes us: What if God should hide his commandments from me one day? I would collapse into nothing; I would stumble and fall at my first step in the strange land.

But now I must ask myself whether I am already guided so much by my own principles that I might not even notice if God withdrew his living commandment from me one day. I might go on acting in accordance with my principles, but God's commandment would no longer be with me. God's commandment is God's personal word to me for this present day, for my day-to-day living. Of course, God's commandment is not today this and tomorrow that, since God's law is at one with itself. But it makes all the difference whether I obey God or my principles. If I am content with my principles, then I cannot understand the prayer of the psalmist. But if I allow myself to be shown the way by God, then I will depend entirely on the grace which is revealed or denied to me; then I will tremble as I receive each word from the mouth of God, because of my need for the next word and for his continuing grace. Thus I will remain in all my ways and my decisions totally bound to grace, and no false security will be able to lure me away from this living fellowship with God.

—Dietrich Bonhoeffer
Meditating on the Word

— HOLY MADNESS —

Silence is the best response to mystery. "There is no way of telling people," Merton reminds us, "that they are all walking around shining like the sun." New Yorkers are told a great many things by strangers on the street, holy fools and mad alike. But the monk's madness is one that shows in the quiet life itself, with its absurd repetition of prayer and liturgy. It is "the madness of great love," in the words of one monk, that "sees God in all things," which nevertheless may be safely and quietly carried out of the monastery, into the world, and back again. As Basil Cardinal Hume, a Benedictine, has remarked, the monk is safe in the marketplace because he is at home in the desert.

—Kathleen Norris
Dakota: A Spiritual Biography

— TEMPTATIONS —

My movement from Harvard to L'Arche made me aware in a new way how much my own thinking about Christian leadership had been affected by the desire to be relevant, the desire for popularity, and the desire for power. Too often I looked at being relevant, popular, and powerful as ingredients of an effective ministry. The truth, however, is that these are not vocations but temptations. Jesus asks, "Do you love me?" Jesus sends us out to be shepherds, and Jesus promises a life in which we increasingly have to stretch out our hands and be led to places where we would rather not go. He asks us to move from a concern for relevance to a life of prayer, from worries about popularity to communal and mutual ministry, and from a leadership built on power to a leadership in which we critically discern where God is leading us and our people.

The people of L'Arche are showing me new ways. I am a slow learner. Old patterns that have proved quite effective are not easy to give up. But as I think about the Christian leader of the next century, I do believe that those from whom I least expected to learn are showing me the way. I hope and pray that what I am learning in my new life is something that is not just good for me to learn, but something that helps you, as well, to catch a glimpse of the Christian leader of the future.

What I have said is, obviously, nothing new, but I hope and pray that you have seen that the oldest, most traditional vision of Christian leadership is still a vision that awaits realization in the future.

I leave you with the image of the leader with outstretched hands, who chooses a life of downward mobility. It is the image of the praying leader, the vulnerable leader, and the trusting leader. May that image fill your hearts with hope, courage, and confidence as you anticipate the next century.

—Henri J. M. Nouwen
In the Name of Jesus

What is this seed that thou hast planted in me
that I must bring to fruit
or pass my life in sterile waste?
What is this gift that thou hast given me
that I must in turn pass on
or it will destroy me?
What is it you are asking me to do
that I must do
or know my life defeated?
I ask, in Christ's name.
Amen.

—Edward Tyler
Prayers in Celebration of the Turning Year

RETREAT  PATTERN

Prayer for Guidance

> Faithful Savior, deliver me from the false impression that I can follow you, love as you did, and live as you did on my own strength. Help me honestly to examine my life in the light of your presence this day. Lead me in these hours beyond self-examination and confession to forgiveness and new life to the end that my life and ministry may be renewed. *Amen.*

Silent Listening

Scripture Reading

> Psalm 51:1-17; Luke 7:36-50; Ephesians 4:1-16; Romans 8:31-39; Hosea 14:1-9; John 21:15-19; Philippians 3:8-16; Matthew 26:20-56
>
> > How do these scriptures address you today?
> > Where do you see yourself in each of these passages?
> > What response do they call forth from your life?

Spiritual Reading

Reflection

Mealtime, Rest, Recreation

Journaling

Prayer

Further Spiritual Reading, Reflection, Journaling, Prayer

Eucharist

Response: Thanksgiving, Offerings, Covenant

Returning to the World

> You may use suggestions from the appendix or design your own plan of faithful living, including daily and weekly actions designed to nurture and sustain your life and ministry.

Closing Prayer

> Giver of every good and perfect gift, once more I desire to offer myself and my ministry to you. Accept the offering I make and lead me in paths of righteousness, goodness, and truth. Guide my life and ministry in the way of faithfulness and fruitfulness. *Amen.*

3.
IN THE MIDST OF FAULTS AND FAILURES

T o be in ministry is to experience failure. At first reading this may seem a harsh and exaggerated statement. But anyone who has sought faithfully to fulfill the call to ministry for even a brief time knows both the feelings and the reality of failure.

Sometimes our faults are imagined and we simply experience feelings of failure. At such a time these feelings should be ignored or driven from our consciousness by careful evaluation and prayer. Unreasonable and unholy expectations that are placed upon us by others and ourselves can easily lead us to feelings of failure and even to despair. Therefore, feelings of failure should be looked in the eye, evaluated, owned, and confronted. We should ask about the root of these feelings. When do they come and from whence do they come and why? Sometimes the exercise of identifying our feelings of failure, coupled with a cry for help in our prayers, is all that it takes to place these unreasonable feelings in the hands of God for transformation and elimination. However, if the feelings persist, without rational basis, and after confession and prayer, it will be wise to seek the help of a trusted spiritual guide.

Unfortunately, feelings of failure often are the mirror reflection of genuine failure, failure that comes at many levels. Sometimes this failure is known only to God and ourselves and at other times it is so very public that it is impossible to hide or ignore. Sometimes this failure is like a dull and distant pain and sometimes the failure is more like a searing, scorching, scarring burn. We may never experience the latter, but we are sure to experience the former.

The only way to avoid the experience of failure is to have such a low image of ministry that any effort, any lifestyle, any level of competency more than meets our expectations. But to see ministry as the response to the call of our faithful Savior, Jesus Christ, is always to have before us the challenge of a fidelity and faithfulness that leads us into a lifetime of reaching for the prize of the upward call of God in Jesus Christ (Phil. 3:12-16).

We, like the apostle Paul, know the reality of our weakness. We often fail to do what we plan to do and often do that which we determine not to do. We need to remind each other that our salvation is in Jesus Christ

61

and not in our works, good or otherwise. We are saved by grace, through faith in God and not by our efforts, no matter how noble or extensive. To seek to walk with God, to reflect daily the presence of Christ in all that we are and do is such a challenge that we will all miss the mark. We live so much less than we know of the gospel and in our honest moments it troubles us and drives us to confession of our failure.

Further, to be about the task of leading others in faithfulness and fidelity to Christ is to experience another kind of failure. To become a servant leader within a congregation is a difficult role and none of us do it very well. We look at the One who did it so perfectly, but the cost seems so prohibitive that we live a timid shadow of the radical faithfulness to which we feel called.

Recently a young pastor told me that he rarely finished preaching a sermon without deep feelings of disappointment—disappointment because he had failed to make clear the gospel, failed to winsomely invite others to faithful discipleship, and failed to communicate the vision that he saw of God's reign.

As we talked it became clear to me that this young pastor worked hard, led a prayerful and responsible life, but the challenge was so great and his expectations so high that his best efforts fell short of the demand he felt his commitment to the gospel placed upon his life. His very best efforts to keep the community of faith attentive and responsive to God were always met with a certain amount of failure. Some of that failure is seen in the slowness of a congregation to become faithful and obedient in their corporate or personal response to the gospel. Some of that failure is seen within as our own incompleteness can no longer be hidden. The failure to do and be what we know in our minds and feel in our hearts is possible is apparent to everyone who examines life in the light of Christ and the gospel.

We are not in ministry for long until we find some correlation between the word of the Lord to Ezekiel and our own experience. Ezekiel said, "They come to you . . . and they sit before you . . . and they hear your words. . . . To them you are like a singer of love songs. . . . They hear what you say but they will not do it" (Ezek. 33:31-32). We often experience our own failure in the failure of those we are sent to serve and lead.

It is also true that some of the sense of failure that is so much a part of our ministry is the result of an uninformed understanding of the Christian life and of ministry itself. We expect too much too soon. While we are called to be perfect as God is perfect, rarely does anyone become instantly mature as a Christian. Our intial turning is but the beginning of a lifelong process of "ripening," a lifetime process of turning toward God, a lifetime process of fashioning a relationship of fidelity with God.

The fruit of the Spirit does not ripen overnight (Gal. 5:22-26). And this fruit is never within the easy grasp of an acquisitive society. The fruit of the Spirit requires our discipline and our concentrated effort. But this fruit is available and maturity in Christ is possible. Each of us has been created to be "filled with all the fullness of God" (Eph. 3:19) and to "live in love as Christ loved us and gave himself up for us" (Eph. 5:1-2).

To the sensitive this awareness of failure can nibble away at our peaceful heart and even our effectiveness in ministry. But there is remedy. There is a "cure for the sinsick soul." It is well to keep this truth in mind when we discuss those times when covenant is shattered by some obvious and horrendous act of infidelity and disobedience. Is there still remedy? The answer is obvious. Of course! Complete cure is guaranteed. It is Jesus who heals the sick, gives sight to the blind, raises the dead, and forgives the sinner.

There is no question of cure. But first there must be examination, confession, and repentance. Richard Foster speaks of the "Prayer of Examen." It is a time when we invite God to scrutinize every facet of our existence. We not only invite the Lord to scrutinize our deepest self, but we ask that the light, the healing light, the purifying light, the life-giving light of Christ's presence touch our deepest failure and our most broken self. Yes, there is remedy for our woundedness. Complete cure is assured.

However, there is no guarantee that all of the scar tissue around the wounds of our broken covenants can be removed. While the scars may be reduced through prayer, love, action, and time itself, the scars still remain. And yet, I remind you that the wounds of infidelity, no matter how deep, may be healed. Even Peter, carrying the burden of denial, was able to hear again the Lord's call and to respond with an answering love before receiving directions for his future ministry (John 21:15-19).

When our failure is such a monumental sin that it threatens to crush us and our ministry, we need to remember that there is remedy, complete remedy for our brokenness. Or, when our failure is the continuing experience of missing the mark of our own expectations, we should remind ourselves that remedy is available to us. And even when we carry the burden of our inability to move a preoccupied people toward faithfulness, we must remember, there is indeed healing, redemption, and renewal available for those who seek to walk with God. That cure is offered in Christ through whom "we have redemption . . . according to the riches of his grace" (Eph. 1:7). We tap into this grace in a great variety of ways. The readings which follow by Holmes and Foster mention some of those ways. This retreat experience is still another opportunity to receive God's healing. Time for reflection, rest, and attention to God is essential to our redemption. Let this be a time of healing for you.

To be burdened with a false feeling of failure is foolish and contrary to what we believe about the gospel. To ignore our sins, deny our need for forgiveness and healing is to choose death over life. We are constantly called to experience the transformation that only God can give. We accept that transformation by walking through the doorway of confession and repentance. Passing through the threshold of repentance helps us to see God's utter and complete faithfulness. In spite of our infidelity and failure God's faithfulness and fidelity remain steadfast (Ps. 59:17). The Scriptures frequently talk of God's steadfast love and nowhere more eloquently than in the story of Hosea or the example of Jesus.

We find remedy for our failures, false and imagined, in God. Our remedy is in the God who made us, chose us before the foundation of the world (Eph. 1), called us to discipleship and to Christian ministry. We have been set aside for specific functions within the church and we share with all sinners a common need of a Savior. The good news of the gospel that we preach to others is also good news to us. Christ died to save sinners and we may receive the healing, redeeming, and saving gift of God even as we spend time on retreat. We may return from this time apart cleansed, forgiven, made whole, and redirected in faithfulness and fidelity.

We want to be better than we are, but often seem unable to move from where we are to where we want to be. Even when our fidelity falters God's fidelity remains. That is the good news that we share with those we lead and it is the good news we must appropriate for ourselves. Our hope is in the One who has the capacity to put a new heart and a new spirit within us (Ezek. 36:26). And this One who is able to put a new spirit and a new heart within us is also able to make us strong to walk in the pathways of fidelity and faithfulness all the days of our lives. Robert Schnase says it well in *Ambition in Ministry:*

> The mystery of God's grace is deeper than we think. It washes away all lesser attainments. Of all God's creatures, only we are cursed with the consciousness of an unreturning past, and only we are privileged to contemplate the end and purpose of life—not just of our own lives or our work, but the end and purpose of life itself. Our perishable accomplishments find their meaning only as we derive it from the eternal presence and imperishable purposes of God. We are saved by grace.

When failure comes, and it is sure to come to all who are in ministry, remember your faithful Savior, Jesus Christ. The redemption offered is adequate for you and me. Do not be reluctant to place your life under the light of Christ for examination. It is a revealing and healing light that brings life and hope. Offer the revealed failures and faults to God with the same abandonment with which you offer yourself. You will discover acceptance and restoration from the hands of the One who made you and loves you. Plan now to establish the way of life and disciplines that can be your counsel and helpers as you seek to walk in fidelity and faithfulness.

May the Holy Spirit grant you strength, power, wisdom, and love to fulfill your calling with faithfulness and joy.

SPIRITUAL  READINGS

— FAITHFUL LOVE —

There are days when I reflect
upon the moments of my history
and I taste satisfied fragrance,
like a well-aged bottle of wine.

It is easy then to ponder
the beauty of Isaiah's God:
holding me in tender arms,
etching my name on divine palms.

There are other long-spent days
when I chew upon my memories,
only to taste the dry crumbs
of stale and molded bread.

How difficult then to perceive
the steadfast love of God;
How empty then is my longing
for a sense of divine embrace.

There are yet other days
when I sit at a great distance,
looking at the life that is mine;
threading the loom of my past
with a deep belief in faithfulness.

It is then that I see how fidelity
has little to do with fine feelings,
and everything to do with deep trust,
believing the One who holds me in joy
will never let go when sorrow steps in.

—Joyce Rupp
May I Have This Dance?

In the Midst of Faults and Failures
— TRUST IN GOD'S FORGIVING LOVE —

One temptation that will haunt us from time to time, and especially on our deathbed, is whether all the sins we have committed in our lifetime have really been forgiven by God. "How can we really be sure?" is a question all of us, perhaps, have asked ourselves. We wonder: Did I confess my sins properly? Didn't I withhold certain sins in confession out of shame? Perhaps I rationalized my way out of certain sins, justifying myself only to be tormented as I grew older by the thought of a possible hell for all eternity as my just due.

Martin Luther, the initiator of the Protestant Reformation in Germany and founder of Lutheranism, was tormented by such scrupulous questionings. He wrote that as an Augustinian monk he was torn by doubts about his own justification and whether he eventually would be saved. He records his "tower experience," when he locked himself up in the tower in the Wittenberg monastery and refused to come down until he received from God the certainty that he was saved by faith in the blood of Jesus and that his sins were truly forgiven.

Perhaps most Christians are in the greatest need of trust in God's forgiveness of their personal sins. We must, for true integration and health of body, soul and spirit, begin always by accepting our past sins and guilt and humbly bring them to God's merciful forgiveness in order to receive from him inner peace and healing.

But our sins can be treated by us in various ways. Some Christians entertain lax consciences and an ability easily to rationalize themselves out of any guilt or need for reform. Such people presume too much about God's mercy. They have read scripture and heard sermons about God's mercy. But they conveniently forget the necessity of a conversion by turning away from living selfishly toward God and neighbor. . . .

Have Mercy on Me, a Sinner

The first step in a true conversion toward integration and coming into a deeper union with God and neighbor in love comes when we have the honesty and courage to confront our brokenness and accept our responsibility for that something which is false, unreal, unauthentic in the way we approach God, in the way we habitually look at ourselves and at others. It is a question we need to ask ourselves, not once, but continually throughout our whole lifetime. "Will I stay inside myself groping for ways in which I can allow God to be truly 'my God' instead of running 'outside' to be diverted from the call of God to new life?"

Gabriel Marcel, the great French philosopher, writes about the need we have of distractions to keep us away from the horrendous task of getting in touch with our sinfulness, guilt and fears:

> When we are at rest, we find ourselves almost inevitably put in the presence of our own inner emptiness, and this very emptiness is in reality intolerable to us. But there is more, there is the fact that through this emptiness we inevitably become aware of the misery of our condition, as "a condition so miserable," says Pascal, "that nothing can console us when we think about it carefully." Hence, the necessity of diversion. (*Problematic Man*, p. 100)

What fears rise up like specters out of the mist and fog of our past! What raw experiences trigger anger, hatred, unforgiveness! What moods of depression, melancholy and loneliness come over us when we reflect on the wasted parts of our life! We see what sinful tendencies lie deep within us, what heinous evil acts we are capable of committing. We see the stranglehold of past habits exercising their enslavement over us. God lets a soft light of what-could-have-been shine into our broken darkness as we see the many areas of omissions, of good deeds not done, of God's gentle whispers unheeded.

With St. Paul we can cry out to God:

> In my inmost self I dearly love God's Law, but I can see that my body follows a different law that battles against the law which my reason dictates. This is what makes me a prisoner of that law of sin which lives inside my body.
>
> What a wretched man I am! Who will rescue me from this body doomed to death? Thanks be to God through Jesus Christ our Lord! (Rom 7:22-25)

Once we have the courage to have a healthy disgust with our eating of "the husks the pigs were eating" (Lk 15:16), we become more open to respond in urgent faith to believe in Jesus Christ as the Savior, who alone can take away our sins. We earnestly begin to trust in God's invitation to come back home and accept his forgiving love.

> Come back to me with all your heart,
> fasting, weeping, mourning.
> Let your hearts be broken, not your garments torn,
> turn to Yahweh your God again,
> for he is all tenderness and compassion,
> slow to anger, rich in graciousness,
> and ready to relent. (Jl 2:12-13) . . .

We Cannot Save Ourselves

How difficult it is for us Westerners, who are like the busy Martha, always anxious about what we must do to be saved. We feel uncomfortable in the role of Mary, as she sat at the feet of the Lord. We seem to be driven to prove we are worthwhile by what we do, by our accomplishments. Yet we forget that our "nature" can never stand independently of God's permeating graces at all times. Every gift, every talent and ability to do comes from God. "It is in him that we live, and move, and exist" (Acts 17:28). St. James exhorts us to recognize God as the source of all good: "It is all that is good, everything that is perfect, which is given us from above; it comes down from the Father of all light" (Jas 1:17).

We cannot do things thinking we can barter ourselves into salvation. We will enter into the healing process called salvation only when we realize we cannot heal ourselves or merit by our works the gift of God's love. Only when a recuperating alcoholic recognizes that he or she has a problem and cannot bring about his or her own healing does a new life begin to open up. Such a new life becomes realized only when there is faith in the healing power of an infinite force of love, God himself, who accepts a person's brokenness and replaces the need for alcohol by new self-esteem in the light of a loving community.

So it is with us all. Only when we crack through our false ego, which insists everything is all right and the others around us are the neurotic ones, can we begin to receive the new and eternal life of God. We, only in God's love and power of the Spirit, can stop living the lie and the illusions that keep us separated from a vengeful God and from our neighbor.

God's Unconditional Love

Then we will begin to open ourselves in earnest to receive God's unconditional love, which is always available and active from God's side. He does not have to come to us. It is we who come to his loving and healing presence. It is we who have to allow his mercy and grace to dissipate the darkness of our fearful self and replace it with our true self in the conscious living, no longer we ourselves, but letting Christ live in us, as St. Paul discovered in his conversion.

When our foolish and false pride is shaken and we enter into a true poverty of spirit or authentic humility, we put ourselves continually into the world of God's forgiving mercy and constant love that knows no end. Then Jesus Christ becomes our sole strength. Our very weaknesses become no longer obstacles, but the point where God meets us in his omnipotence, omniscience and omnipresence. St. Paul summarized this essential characteristic at the heart of every true and ongoing conversion before the strength of God's forgiving love

> So I shall be very happy to make my weaknesses my special boast so that the power of Christ may stay over me, and that is why I am quite content with my weaknesses, and with persecutions, and the agonies I go through for Christ's sake. For it is when I am weak that I am strong. (2 Cor 12:9-10) . . .

69

Prayer of Forgiveness. Heavenly Father, in awe and reverence I fall before your majesty, holiness, beauty and goodness. You are the snow-capped mountain on which the gazelle and the young stag joyfully leap and bound. I am a darkened desert valley in which there is no beauty, but what flashes as brilliant light from you into my nothingness.

O Father, your child is sad and filled with tears. I am frightened as I crouch in the depths of darkness and despair. Fears and anxious worries, like bats shearing wildly through a confining cave, beat my soul. The evil in my heart clutches around my throat. I gasp for your life-giving breath as my sinfulness covers me with the cloak of death.

There is no place to go but to cry out in my despearate search to look upon your face. My spirit, like parched earth, cries out to you, my heavenly Father, for your healing mercy, your forgiving love!

Send me your forgiving Voice, your Word made flesh, Jesus, my Savior, to speak in stillness deep as summer fields kept windless in the blazing sun of noon and silvered in the silence of the night, and yet as loud as thunder. May his Spirit come upon me as healing Love, that I may receive your forgiveness. . . .

Lord, Jesus Christ, let me hear you command me as you did the entombed Lazarus, "Come out!" I pray earnestly that your forgiving love will unbind me and set me free. I believe, for me you have died. Looking into your blood-covered face as you hang dying on the cross, I sob for your forgiveness. As the soft morning dawn gently lifts the darkness from the face of the earth to let the sun burst into being with full radiance, so let the light of the Father's love softly fall upon my broken spirit to drive away the darkness of despair and abandonment.

I know in my brokenness I cannot buy or merit your forgiveness of my many sins. I believe you are Love by your nature, always present with warm love, ever covering me as rays of summer sun drive out all coldness of limb.

I need only to walk out of my coldness and darkness into your loving presence to receive your new life. Gather up into your mighty arms my past sins and, like fire touching sun-dried straw in the fields, burn up into vanishing smoke my sinfulness and leave me purified by your forgiving love.

Lord Jesus, you are the Father's mercy in my miseries. In you I trust that I am forgiven all my sins. In you I believe I can begin a new life. In you there is no longer any condemnation. Your love has set me free!

Loving Father, let me hear you say to your prodigal child, who asks your forgiveness, the beautiful and consoling words Jesus spoke in the Gospel parable: "We are going to have a feast, a celebration, because this child of mine was dead and has come back to life; he was lost and is found" (Lk 15:23-24).

Jesus! Abba! I trust in you because you truly love me!

—George A. Maloney
In Jesus We Trust

— TO FAIL MORE OFTEN —

If we are truly people of faith, we must be willing to fail more often. If we fail infrequently, it means we are not acting boldly enough or lovingly enough, enough of the time. It means we are hiding behind walls of past successes and shrinking from present-day risks which will determine what is possible. Unless we fail on a regular basis, God will have insufficient raw material with which to work. It is from our haphazard efforts that the Holy One can sculpt works of art.

So be unafraid. Dare to fail more often!

—Hope Douglas J. Harle-Mould
Church Worship

— THE SHAPE OF PASTORAL INTEGRITY —

The biblical fact is that there are no successful churches. There are, instead, communities of sinners, gathered before God week after week in towns and villages all over the world. The Holy Spirit gathers them and does his work in them. In these communities of sinners, one of the sinners is called pastor and given a designated responsibility in the community. The pastor's responsibility is to keep the community attentive to God. It is this responsibility that is being abandoned in spades.

"Hot indignation seizes me . . ." (Ps. 119:53). I don't know how many share my anger. I know a few names. Altogether there can't be very many of us. Are there yet seven thousand who have not bowed the knee to Baal? Are there enough to be identifiable as a minority? I think so. We recognize each other from time to time. And much has been accomplished by minorities. And there must be any number of shopkeepers who by now are finding the pottage that they acquired in exchange for their ordination birthright pretty tasteless stuff and are growing wistful for a restoration to their calling. Is the wistfulness an ember strong enough to blaze into a fierce repudiation of their defection, allowing the word of God again to become fire in their mouths? Can my anger apply a bellows to those coals?

Three pastoral acts are so basic, so critical, that they determine the shape of everything else. The acts are praying, reading Scripture, and giving spiritual direction. Besides being basic, these three acts are quiet. They do not call attention to themselves and so are often not attended to. In the clamorous world of pastoral work nobody yells at us to engage in these acts. It is possible to do pastoral work to the satisfaction of the people who judge our competence and pay our salaries without being either diligent or skilled in them. Since almost never does anyone notice whether we do these things or not, and only occasionally does someone ask that we do them, these three acts of ministry suffer widespread neglect.

The three areas constitute acts of attention: prayer is an act in which I bring myself to attention before God: reading Scripture is an act of attending to God in his speech and action across two millennia in Israel and Christ: spiritual direction is an act of giving attention to what God is doing in the person who happens to be before me at any given moment.

Always it is God to whom we are paying, or trying to pay, attention. The contexts, though, vary: in prayer the context is myself; in Scripture it is the community of faith in history; in spiritual direction it is the person before me. God is the one to whom we are being primarily attentive in these contexts, but it is never God-in-himself; rather, it is God-in-relationship—with me, with his people, with this person.

None of these acts is public, which means that no one knows for sure whether or not we are doing any of them. People hear us pray in worship, they listen to us preach and teach from the Scriptures, they notice when we are listening to them in a conversation, but they can never know if we are attending to *God* in any of this. It doesn't take many years in this business to realize that we can conduct a fairly respectable pastoral ministry without giving much more than ceremonial attention to God. Since we can omit these acts of attention without anybody noticing, and because each of the acts involves a great deal of rigor, it is easy and common to slight them.

This is not entirely our fault. Great crowds of people have entered into a grand conspiracy to eliminate prayer, Scripture, and spiritual direction from our lives. They are concerned with our image and standing, with what they can measure, with what produces successful church-building programs and impressive attendance charts, with sociological impact and economic viability. They do their best to fill our schedules with meetings and appointments so that there is time for neither solitude nor leisure to be before God, to ponder Scripture, to be unhurried with another person.

We get both ecclesiastical and community support in conducting a ministry that is inattentive to God and therefore without foundations. Still, that is no excuse. A professional, by some definitions, is someone who is committed to standards of integrity and performance that cannot be altered to suit people's tastes or what they are willing to pay for. Professionalism is in decline these days on all fronts—in medicine, in law, in politics, as well as among pastors—but it has not yet been repudiated. There are still a considerable number of professionals in all areas of life who do the hard work of staying true to what they were called to do, stubbornly refusing to do the easy work that the age asks of them. . . .

The image aspects of being a pastor, the parts that have to do with meeting people's expectations, can be faked easily. We can impersonate a pastor without being a pastor. The problem, though, is that while we can get by with it in our communities, often with applause, we can't get by with it within ourselves. At least not all of us. Some of us get restive. We feel awful. No level of success seems to be proof against an eruption of *angst* in the middle of our applauded performance. The restiveness does not come from Puritan guilt: we *are* doing what we are paid to do. The people who pay our salaries are getting their money's worth. We are "giving good weight"—the sermons are inspiring, the committees are efficient, the morale is good. The restiveness comes from another dimension—from a vocational memory, a spiritual hunger, a professional commitment. Being the kind of pastor that satisfies a congregation is one of the easiest jobs on the face of the earth—*if* we are satisfied with satisfying congregations. The hours are good, the pay is adequate, the prestige is considerable. Why don't we find it easy? Why aren't we content with it?

Because we set out to do something quite different. We set out to risk our lives in a venture of faith. We committed ourselves to a life of holiness. At some point we realized the immensity of God and of the great invisibles that socket into our arms and legs, into bread and wine, into our brains and our tools, into mountains and rivers giving them meaning, destiny, value, joy, beauty, salvation. We responded to a call to convey these realities in word and sacrament and to give leadership to a community of faith in such a way that connected and coordinated what the men and women, children and youth in this community are doing in their work and play with what God is doing in mercy and grace. In the process we learned the difference between a profession or craft, and a job. . . .

We all start out knowing this, or at least having a pretty good intimation of it. But when we entered our first parish we were given a job. Most of the people that we deal with most of the time are dominated by a sense of self, not a sense of God. Insofar as we also deal with their primary concern, the self—directing, counseling, instructing, encouraging—they give us good marks in our jobs as pastors. Whether we deal with God or not, they don't care overly much. Flannery O'Connor describes one pastor in such circumstances as one part minister and three parts masseuse.

It is very difficult to do one thing when most of the people around us are asking us to do something quite different, especially when these people are nice, intelligent, treat us with respect, and pay our salaries. We get up each morning and the telephone rings, people meet us, letters are addressed to us—often at a tempo of bewildering urgency. All of these calls and people and letters are from people who are asking us to do something for them, quite apart from any belief in God. That is, they come to us not because they are looking for God but because they are looking for a recommendation, or good advice, or an opportunity, and they vaguely suppose that we might be qualified to give it to them. . . .

Am I keeping the line clear between what I am committed to and what people are asking of me? Is my primary orientation God's grace, his mercy, his action in creation and covenant? And am I committed enough to it so that when people ask me to do something that will not lead them into a more mature participation in these realities and actions I refuse? I don't like to think of all the visits I have made, counseling given, marriages performed, meetings attended, prayers offered—one friend calls it sprinkling holy water on Cabbage Patch dolls—solely because people asked me to do it and it didn't seem at the time that it would do any harm and who knows it might do some good. Besides, I knew there was a pastor down the street who would do anything asked of him but whose theology was so wretched that he would probably do active harm in the process. My theology, at least, was evangelical and orthodox.

How do I keep the line sharp? How do I maintain a sense of pastoral vocation in the middle of a community of people who are hiring me to do religious jobs? How do I keep a sense of professional integrity in the midst of a people who are long practiced in comparative shopping and who don't get overly exercised on the fine points of pastoral integrity?

There is an old and good answer to these questions. It is not one-liner advice but immersion in a subject that used to be the core curriculum in the formation of pastors and priests. The subject went under the name of ascetical theology, what I am calling "working the angles." . . .

Without an adequate "ascetic" the best of talents and best of intentions cannot prevent a thinning out into a life that becomes mostly impersonation.

If the pastors of America were asked two questions, "What do you think about God?" and "What do you want to accomplish as a pastor?" I believe that a great majority of answers would have to be judged satisfactory. But what if we are asked a third question. "How do you go about it—what *means* do you use to bring your spiritual goals into being in your parish?" At this point the responses would range, I am quite sure, from the faddish to the trite to the silly. Pastors, by and large, have not lost touch with the best thinking about God, and they have not lost touch with the high goals of the Christian life, but they have lost touch with the trigonometry of ministry, the angles, the *means* by which the lines of the work get connected into a triangle, *pastoral* work. The pastor who has no facility in *means* buys games and gimmicks and programs without end under the illusion of being practical.

So. There is a readily available theology of ministry. We have a well-intentioned ministry. But we have an impoverished technology of ministry. Martin Thornton tells us that when he gets through reading a book on ministry he usually finds its margins littered with the initials YBH: "Yes, but how?" Terrific ideas! Excellent thinking! Superb insights! Great goals! "Yes, but how?" How do I go about it? What are the actual means by which I carry out this pastoral vocation, this ordained ministry, this professional commitment to God's word and God's grace in my life and the lives of the people to whom I preach and give the sacraments, among whom I command a life for others in the name of Jesus Christ? What connects these great realities of God and the great realities of salvation to the geography of this parish and in the chronology of this week? The answer among the masters whom I consult doesn't change: a trained attentiveness to God in prayer, in Scripture reading, in spiritual direction. This has not been tried and discarded because it didn't work, but tried and found difficult (and more than a little bit tedious) and so shelved in favor of something or other that could be fit into a busy pastor's schedule.

It is common among us to hear these areas of practiced attentiveness to God in the three foundational contexts slighted on the grounds that "I have no aptitude for that sort of thing" or "My interests lie in another field." The fact is that nobody has an aptitude for it. It is hard work. It is unglamorous work. I have spent a considerable amount of time for much of my life among track and field athletes: I have never met one who liked to run laps or do pushups. But I have met a few who were determined to win races and some who had a great desire to break records. They accepted whatever practices their coaches assigned to them so that they could do their very best with the bodies they had and so attain these excellent ends. The pastor's coaches are the spiritual/ascetical theologians. They work across a vast spectrum of cultural conditions and represent every conceivable aptitude and temperament. These people resist categorization, are impatient with labels and formulas, and continually catch us off guard with one surprise after another. They insist that there are "no dittos among souls," whether in pastors or the people they work with. Still, underlying the flourishing of spontaneities is a pervasive consensus that none of us can mature into excellence without a lifelong persistence of trained attentiveness to God in the soul, in Israel and church, and in the neighbor as we work away at our trigonometry of prayer, Scripture, and spiritual direction.

—Eugene H. Peterson
Working the Angles

— THE IRONY OF OUR PREDICAMENT —

J. F. Powers's *Morte D'Urban* tells the story of a fictitious Father Urban Roche, a talented go-getter in an equally fictitious declining religious order, the Clementines. Father Urban chafes under the uninspired leadership of his religious superiors. *He* knows how to make the Clementines succeed. His golden opportunity comes when he is put in charge of a floundering retreat center. By purchasing an adjoining golf course, he figures out a way to provide the necessary revenue.

Urban's compromise is hilarious—until I stop to realize that I am prone to the same temptation. I work in a religious bureaucracy that struggles daily with the same dilemma: how to keep the bureaucratic machinery going without betraying the gospel we profess to proclaim. Clergy in the local church face the same dilemma: how to make a parish church successful without becoming unfaithful in the pursuit of that success. Powers is not particularly judgmental. But he does lay bare the irony of our situation. We *are* lost souls if we no longer feel uncomfortable with the irony of our predicament.

—Jack A. Keller, Jr.
Quarterly Review

— TURNING INWARD —

Earlier I said that the Prayer of Examen had two aspects. That is accurate enough in analysis, but when we come to practice, it can be misleading. In reality, the experience is more like an animated computer graphic of two concentric circles that are constantly overlapping, interfacing, and weaving into and out of one another. We watch, for example, for God's activity in our lives, and when we find it we discover that he has exposed our blind side. The examen of consciousness and the examen of conscience are a little like the waves of the ocean: distinct from one another and yet constantly on top of and never totally separate from each other. Understanding this, we now turn to *the* question: how do we practice the Prayer of Examen?

We practice it by turning inward. Not outward, not upward, but inward. Anthony Bloom writes, "Your prayer must be turned inwards, not towards a God of Heaven nor towards a God far off, but towards God who is closer to you than you are aware."

With examen more than any other form of prayer, we bore down deeper and deeper, the way a drill would bore down into the bowels of the earth. We are constantly turning inward—but inward in a very special way. I do not mean to turn inward by becoming ever more introspective, nor do I mean to turn inward in hopes of finding within ourselves some special inner strength or an inner savior who will deliver us. Vain search! No, it is not a journey *into* ourselves that we are undertaking but a journey *through* ourselves so that we can emerge from the deepest level of the self into God. As Saint John Chrysostom notes, "Find the door of your heart, you will discover it is the door of the kingdom of God."

Madame Guyon calls this special kind of inward turning "the law of central tendency." "As you continue holding your soul deep in your inward parts, you will discover that God has a *magnetic* attracting quality! Your God is like a magnet! The Lord naturally draws you more and more toward Himself." We are drawn into the Divine Center, says Guyon, through God's grace rather than by our own efforts. She concludes, "Your soul, once it begins to turn inward, is brought under this . . . law of central tendency. It . . . gradually falls toward its proper center, which is God. The soul needs no other force to draw it than the weight of love."

—Richard Foster
Prayer

— THE SINS OF THE CLERGY —

The Fathers of the early church who went out into the desert are popularly thought to have been fleeing the evils of civilization. But this is a simplification. They thought of themselves more properly as going out to fight evil. The demons, as well as the angels, were believed to live in the wilderness and there could be confronted and bested in all their horrible destructiveness.

The besetting sin of the desert fathers was acedia or *accidie*, tellingly described as "the devil of the noonday sun." Acedia is spiritual boredom, an indifference to matters of religion, or simple laziness. Symeon the New Theologian wrote to his monks, "Do not forget your special tasks and your handicraft to walk about aimlessly and in dissipation and so expose yourselves to the demon of accidie." His remark is almost a commentary on the axiom, "Idle hands are the devil's workshop."

The ancient sin of acedia lies at the root of the pastor's or priest's refusal to heed the calling to be the instrument of spiritual growth. In 1977 Carlyle Marney, a distinguished Baptist "pastor to pastors," spoke at the seminary where I serve. I remember him asking our students if they thought after ten years they would still love the Lord Jesus or if instead would have become "hand tamed by the gentry." Of course, he would have been exceedingly surprised if any had confessed that probably the latter would be the case, but the fact is that many ordained persons quickly lose a sense of the excitement of the spiritual quest. They succumb to acedia in those forms that are to a degree peculiar to our times, and yet share much with previous centuries of clergy.

Many of us when we think of the sins of the clergy recall the "fallen priest" in literature, such as the Reverend T. Lawrence Shannon in Tennessee Williams' play, *The Night of the Iguana*. He was a boozer, a wencher, and had lost his faith. Yet, such a person is less a sinner than he is a casualty. American religion is obsessed with the "warm sins" such as illicit sex and gluttony. Because many of us are Donatists—believing that the validity of the sacrament depends upon the moral character of its minister, which was condemned as a heresy long ago—we become inordinately concerned when the warm sins are committed by the ordained. What we fail to realize is that pastor or priest who succumbs to the sins of passion is fallen in the same manner as a fallen soldier. These are the demons that threaten anyone who sets out upon the path through chaos. Some will lose.

The sins that should concern us far more deeply are those that prevent the ordained from ever exercising their spiritual vocation. These "cold sins" truly violate the mission of the pastor to be a symbol, symbol-bearer, and hermeneut. They arise not from an excess of passion, but from a fear of passion. They are the product of a calculated apathy, sustained only by the embers of a dying soul.

Acedia is the root sin of the clergy as spiritual guides. Like a cancer it eats away at our abandonment to the love for God and his creation. It takes a number of forms, which have much in common with those of other centuries but also have their own peculiar twist in our times.

The Lust for Power

Everyone needs to possess power. Power is the ability to change situations and circumstances. The issue is not the fact of power per se, but rather the nature and source of that power.

The Greek word for power, *dunamis* (we get the word "dynamite" from it), is common in the New Testament, as is a word for authority, *exousia,* which is sometimes translated as power. There power is of God and is given to the church that creation might become whole. Jesus before his ascension tells the apostles, "You will receive power when the Holy Spirit comes upon you; and you will bear witness for me . . . away to the ends of the earth" (Acts 1:8). Paul declares that the Gospel "is the saving power of God for everyone who has faith" (Rom 1:16). Christ, he tells us, "is the power and the wisdom of God" (1 Cor. 1:24). The juxtaposition of power *(dunamis)* and wisdom *(sophia)* is not coincidental here. *Sophia* is feminine and the power of *exousia* is related to a feminine consciousness. . . .

At a clergy conference typical of a number of such gatherings, I recall making the point that the spiritual life is necessarily subversive of our fondest assumptions about ourselves, and also making the additional point that the people of the church claim that they want someone of spiritual depth as their pastor. I was confronted on this with some bitterness by a priest who questioned the sincerity of people who claim they want a pastor of spiritual depth and yet act as if that is the last thing they want. He said, speaking out of experience, "If spirituality is fundamentally subversive, it will not get you elected bishop."

There are other ways to power in the church and many seek them. One of the persons interviewed, a quiet, scholarly, Roman Catholic priest, spoke sadly and yet firmly to me of his decision to avoid where possible clerical gatherings at which his bishop and the chancellor were present. The sycophancy of the clergy, he explained, left him ill and life is too short to suffer that. I have seen the same behavior toward ecclesiastical superiors at other gatherings—Episcopal, Methodist, Baptist—so no denomination has a corner on that market. Another Roman Catholic priest spoke to me of his amazement at hearing a bishop speak of himself as being "at this point in my career." What, he asked, does that mean? Is it true that if a bishop comes into a small diocese and does his work well and "keeps his nose clean" that he may advance higher? What does "higher" mean, he inquired? What has happened, he went on, to a sense of vocation?

External power comes with the acquisition of role and status. There is an interesting play on the power from within and the power that comes with rank in the story of the centurion who comes to Jesus to ask him to heal his servant (Matt. 8:5-10). The centurion uses the analogy of his own power to suggest that Jesus can heal at long distance by virtue of Jesus' power. Of course, the power is of a different kind. Jesus' is *exousia,* from the very nature of his being, while the centurion's is external. . . .

I do not believe that most persons seek ordination in order to get advancement in the church. There are career ladders with greater reward. The personality profiles I have seen only confirm the opinion that the vast majority of individuals responding to the call tend toward the end of the spectrum that holds dreamers, visionaries, and thinkers rather than the end that produces politicians, entrepreneurs, and go-getters. But they are taught that if they are to educate their children, live in reasonable comfort, maintain a car, enjoy even a modicum of the material wealth of our country, they must "pay the piper and dance to his tune." This is how the quest for external power is promoted. The lust for power never quite gets so preoccupying that in the early morning hours there is not a sinking feeling that something has been lost.

Yet it becomes all too easy to justify a ministry that regularly requires us to "belly up" to the bar at the local country club. We become a part of that ongoing power play that feeds the "messianic grandeur," as one pastor put it, that afflicts some clergy. It is difficult to discover what in this style of life fits the Gospel of Jesus Christ, but we can become inured to its judgment.

Crucifixion is no symbol of success in late twentieth-century America. Yet, control is certainly an indication of being somebody. So there is a satisfaction in having a power over others that does not require us to face suffering, failure, and an honest appraisal of our own unworthiness, rather than the power of wisdom, which requires this and more. The professional model of ministry has encouraged us to think that this external power of control is what ministry is all about. To control our "clients," to control our "careers," to control our "certification" as professionals are all objectives in which the society persistently socializes the pastor or priest. As the centurion said of himself, "I say to one, 'Go,' and he goes; to another, 'Come here,' and he comes." Those are the words of a "professional" but have little to do with vocation.

The very thing that is true of the Gospel contradicts those who would achieve political success in the church by being inoffensive. "We proclaim Christ," says Paul, "—yes, Christ nailed to the cross; . . . a stumbling block [skandalon] to Jews and folly to Greeks" (1 Cor. 1:23). It is the scandal of the Gospel that breaks open our presuppositions and enables us to be open to the Word of God. It is this scandal that makes the Christian faith so exciting, so different from acedia. It is to the nonthreatening, wishy-washy pastor or priest, just as to the church in Laodicea, that John the Elder wrote, "Because you are lukewarm, neither hot nor cold, I will spit you out of my mouth" (Rev. 3:16). . . .

The problem of pastoral burnout is an important concern today in ministry studies. It can be defined as vocational exhaustion, the depletion of resources to fulfill one's responsibilities. Pastoral burnout can be faced honestly and remedial action taken, or it can be like a hidden cancer among the ordained. When admitted it is a form of battle wound, when hidden it becomes a form of acedia that manifests itself in insulation and evasion.

The sin that leads to pastoral burnout is like a two-edged sword—it cuts two ways. What gets the pastor into the problem is the temptation to evade his or her own spiritual emptiness by becoming as busy as possible. . . .

The Fear of Failure

At the root of acedia and clerical sins of un-passion lies the fear of failure.

It has become the practice in some dioceses within the Episcopal Church to interview a selected group of priests who are willing to be nominated for bishop in that diocese. In one such selection process a question was asked of the candidates: "How do you handle failure?" One man, a demonstrably successful cardinal rector, probably lost the election on the basis of his answer to that question alone, which was, "I don't recall ever having failed."

How can we serve a Lord, the symbol of whose failure is above our altars, on top of our churches, on our stationery, and around our necks, and claim to be a stranger to failure? The power of Christ's Passion is that every human being can identify with it, if he or she just gives it some thought. Despite our best intentions and our fervent hopes, each of us is nailed to his or her cross daily. Certainly this is true of the ordained person, who is called to be "another Christ" and to risk living by values that the world not only rejects but perceives as subversive of its goals and objectives.

In interviewing persons for this study I noticed something curious about reactions to the question of what failure means in their spiritual life. It was one of the two questions—the other had to do with sexuality—of which they frequently wanted clarification. I myself have found this section difficult to write. I think back over my own twenty-seven years as an ordained priest and I realize that I left one place to go to another saying that the job I came to do I had done. But what if I have to leave a place having failed? What do I make of that? I simply prefer not to think about it.

There were notable exceptions to this resistance to failure. One priest spoke to the issue quite eloquently, "It can be," he said, "an excellent runway for the plane [of spiritual growth] to take off on. . . ." In the American society failure is taboo, so we cover everything up, including death, "because I think we regard death as the supreme failure." Death in all its forms is looked upon as failure and failure is to be avoided at all costs. But the spiritual life is an act of dying to self.

It has almost become a cliché that the ordained person is not called to be successful, but to be faithful. Fidelity requires above all an openness that leaves us terribly vulnerable. Every effort to protect that vulnerability requires us to deny our vocation. Consequently we are called to bear within ourselves the failure of the world to subsist on its own and to carry within ourselves the pain of the cross, even the death of God's son.

A faithful priest spoke to me a day or so after the death of a friend. As he put it, there was no person in this world to whom he was closer. At age forty-two one Saturday afternoon his friend dropped dead without warning, leaving his wife and two teenage children. The priest had rushed to the hospital only to be there in time to assist at the last rites. Then he dissolved into the arms of his friend's wife and with her wept like a baby. Had he failed, he asked me? No, he had celebrated the failure of life as only a priest could, in mourning and in hope.

It is the fear of celebrating the world's failure—ourselves included—that leaves clergy persons in their cold sins. We are in fact called to be magnificent failures, for which only the dying will give us thanks.

—Urban T. Holmes III
Spirituality for Ministry

— A TOUCH OF GENTLENESS —

Without pursuing all the anthropological and theological nuances of self-cruelty, let me suggest something very, very simple. You know what tenderness is. We all have experiences of gentleness and kindness. Think of something that makes you feel that way: perhaps being with a loved one who is suffering, of seeing a small child asleep—whatever calls forth from you a feeling of warmth and tenderness or just simple caring. Feel that feeling. You can do that, almost without trying. It is a very familiar feeling, well known to you. Can you now, just for a moment, feel that way towards yourself?

I am not encouraging you to try to maintain a steady state of self-love, but simply to bring a little kindness toward yourself from time to time. Just an instant of it, just a brief interior touch. This is what gentleness means, and it is in this good atmosphere that your basic sanity can grow. The feeling of kindness towards yourself will probably disappear quickly and be replaced by some old, harsh ridigity. That is all right. When you think of it again, when it again is possible, you can recall it. For God's sake, do not throw upon yourself the extra burden of "having" to feel kindly toward yourself. It's just in the moment, just in the instant, a little touch of gentleness, like a feather.

—Gerald G. May
Simply Sane

— *THE LOVE OF GOD* —

We all expect to love our neighbor from the day we become Christian, and we also expect to love God. Unfortunately, our expectations usually have almost nothing to do with what happens. Many of us have no sense of God at all, or if we do, it is more like a sense of duty or even fear toward God. Then, because we believe we should love God, we judge ourselves to be religious failures.

Our ancestors made no such assumptions about Christian love. Gregory of Nyssa, for example, characterized the life of the monk in three stages. At the beginning, he or she serves God out of fear, like a slave; next, the service of God stems from the desire for a reward, like that of a hired hand. Only in the final stage does this person serve God out of friendship with God, or out of the pure love of God, as a child of God's household. The significant point here for us is that the love of God is conceived of as being *difficult,* something to be learned over a very long time. In fact, this is what ascetic discipline was designed to do: to train its practitioners in the ways of God, so that, if God should put that love into their hearts, they might come truly to love God and God's images, other people.

This belief about the relationship between love of God and of humanity and the training for this love was much older than monasticism. It is still one of the most potentially significant lessons the ancient church has to teach us today. If we should come to understand what it was about and believe it as well, our Christianity would be more realistic, and at the same time it would remove from our shoulders a lot of self-condemnation and unwitting hypocrisy.

—Roberta C. Bondi
To Love as God Loves

— *PRAYER IS THE SOUL'S HOME* —

All things have a home, the bird has a nest, the fox has a hole, the bee has a hive. A soul without prayer is a soul without a home. Weary, sobbing, the soul after roving, roaming through a world pestered with aimlessness, falsehoods, absurdities, seeks a moment in which to gather up its scattered trivialized life, in which to divest itself of enforced pretensions and camouflage; in which to simplify complexities, in which to call for help without being a coward—such a home is prayer. Continuity, permanence, intimacy, authenticity, earnestness are its attributes. For the soul, home is where the prayer is.

Everybody must build his own home; everybody must guard the independence and the privacy of his prayers. It is the source of security for the integrity of conscience, for whatever inkling we attain of eternity.

At home I have a father who judges and cares, who has regard for me, and when I fail and go astray, misses me. I will never give up my home.

What is a soul without prayer? A soul runaway or a soul evicted from its own home.

How marvelous is my home. I enter as a suppliant and emerge as a witness; I enter as a stranger and emerge as next of kin. I may enter spiritually shapless, inwardly disfigured, and emerge wholly changed. It is in moments of prayer that my image is forged, that my striving is fashioned.

To understand the world you must love your home. It is difficult to perceive luminosity anywhere, if there is no light in my home. It is in the light of prayer's radiance that I find my way in the dark. It is prayer that illumines my way.

—Abraham J. Heschel
Tempo

— HAVE COURAGE —

Claim for yourself the courage to be; Yahweh has
   known your particular grief, God has atoned for
   all your guilt.
In the midst of human failure, as mortality admits
   defeat, God's banner advances to ultimate victory.
From the midst of a rag-tag army of saints, the Holy
   One calls to you: "Press on, my perfect, imperfect
   note in the symphony of redemption!"
—Martin Bell
Street Singing and Preaching

IN THE MIDST OF FAULTS AND FAILURES

God of second chances and new beginnings, I am always amazed that you choose to use me for your Kingdom purposes. You use me as I am: imperfect, flawed, ordinary, tending sometimes not to do my best, prone to error, and very inclined to trip and fall.

Always, your grace is greater than my mistakes and stumblings. Thank you, O God, for using me in spite of myself!

Unfailing God, remind me often that, in your sight, failure is never final. By your grace, enable me to deal with my own failures constructively and with the failures of others patiently. Let it be so. *Amen.*

—Trudy Archambeau

RETREAT  PATTERN

Prayer for Guidance

> Loving God, lead me during these hours of retreat to find a healthy balance between being and doing. Set me free from the bondage of unrealistic expectations and fill me with your enabling presence this very day. I offer my prayer in the name of Jesus Christ whose life was a perfect balance of doing and being. *Amen.*

Silent Listening

Scripture Reading

> Luke 10:38-42; John 6:22-40; Matthew 22:34-40; Psalm 121; Matthew 25:1-13, 14-30, 31-46
>
> > How do these passages illumine the tension you feel between being and doing?
> > What way of life is suggested by these passages?

Spiritual Reading

Reflection

Mealtime, Rest, Recreation

Journaling

Prayer

Further Spiritual Reading, Reflection, Journaling, Prayer

Eucharist

Response: Thanksgiving, Offering, Covenant

Returning to the World

> You may use suggestions from the Appendix or design your own plan of faithful living, including daily and weekly actions designed to nurture and sustain your life and ministry.

Closing Prayer

> Accept, O Lord, the offering of life and ministry as I abandon myself to your care and keeping. Be for me guide, sustenance, companion, Savior, and Lord. By your intervention in my life help me to be your faithful disciple. *Amen.*

4.
THE TENSION BETWEEN DOING AND BEING

C onsider it a gift when you keenly feel the tension between doing and being. It is a positive sign of your awareness of God's call, a sign of your maturity in Christ, and one of the places where every Christian minister may experience significant growth and renewal.

The tension between being and doing can be a pressure point of pain and anguish in a sensitive and sincere pastor's heart. We are often troubled and wonder why there never seems to be enough time or energy to pray *and* do. This tension is often ignored, avoided, denied, or covered up. It is better that the tension be recognized, attended to, and even honored for the fertile place of growth it can be. We struggle because compassion for others compels us to act while desire for intimacy with God compels us to flee into solitude.

To achieve a healthy balance here is to have discovered one of the keys of faithful and fruitful ministry. There is strong temptation to deny the tension and, therefore, to fall into patterns of behavior that give attention to only one part of our formation. To recognize the invitation of Jesus to follow this one pathway that includes intimacy and action, prayer and compassion, can help save us from the destructive practice of paying attention to only part of our formation in Christ.

Whether serving a small membership congregation, a mega church, or a five-point circuit, pastors are always pulled in two important directions. One is the direction of doing. Every parish and every community is need-filled enough to demand more time and energy than any pastor can possibly provide. It is these very same needs that drive pastors to their knees seeking God's help for those within their care. It is these very same needs that drive pastors to their knees seeking God's strength for their part in God's active redemption of the world. Recognizing that Christian ministry can be lonely, demanding, and even destructive, faithful pastors are driven to their knees seeking intimacy, healing, and strength that can only come from close companionship with God.

Finding a healthy balance between doing and being is a lifelong journey. It never becomes easy and it never becomes simple. But there are some marks along the pathway that have been left by those who have travelled ahead of us. We are not the first ones to experience this tension.

The disciples returned from their first missionary journey to hear Jesus invite them to "come away to a deserted place all by yourselves and rest a while" (Mark 6:31). And they followed Jesus to a deserted place by themselves for rest, renewal, and prayer. But before their time of rest grew very long, the needs of others burst upon them in dramatic ways. And because Jesus had compassion on the crowds, they were once again thrust into doing (Mark 6:34-44). How like the experience of those who follow Jesus today! Always the invitation to rest and renewal in God comes to those who follow Jesus. Equally certain is the invitation to mission in the world.

A remarkably gifted pastor had completed two faithful pastorates and was now assigned to begin a new congregation. Over a period of years Curtis had learned how to balance the pressures of doing and being in a medium-sized congregation. The needs were great, but there were others to help and there were still others who recognized the importance of nurturing the soul, even—or perhaps especially—for pastors. But now, a few years into the development of a new congregation, all the demands of the parish seemed to come to the pastor. There was no staff to help carry the load, and most of the members and participants in this new congregation were, themselves, new to the faith and new to the church. Therefore, they were unaware of the demands placed upon their pastor and the struggle that was going on in his own heart. His deep awareness of the need for time and space for reflection and prayer was pushing hard against the sometimes desperate needs of the people within his care. How fortunate he was to see clearly both sides of the life of faithful ministry.

It is easy to see only one side. To be so caught up in doing that we forget our doing is in response to our companionship with Christ. Or, to be so caught up in our being, our inner world, that we miss the cry of a needy world for comfort, hope, healing, and life. To see, to feel, and to know this wound of tension between being and doing is a gift from God. It is a wound that is often used to bring us closer to God and send us more dramatically on God's mission in the world.

This pastor took the important first step of recognizing and identifying the tension. And then he took an essential next step in determining to deal creatively and faithfully with the tension. Before long he was meeting regularly with a spiritual director and he had taken control of his schedule and determined that every day would include the rhythm of prayer, action, and reflection. Did the tension go away? Not at all. But the tension became a meeting place with God. The tension became a place of growing sensitivity to a more holistic ministry of contemplation and action. The intersection of being and doing became the place of fruitful formation in this pastor's life and ministry.

Helen was in her first year as senior pastor of a large and active congregation. As I listened to her story, I began to feel the pressures she felt from congregation, spouse, community, and family to fulfill a role uniquely fitted to each of those seeking to shape her life and ministry. I left our conversation convinced that the struggle to be her true self was fought in a larger and more risky arena than most of us who are males will ever experience. And yet, the answer to the question, "Who am I?" was found for her as it is for all of us in our faithful savior, Jesus Christ. It was in remembering who God is that she discovered anew who she was as a Christian minister. This discovery made it possible for her to express her true self as pastor, mother, wife, and community leader.

It was these very struggles that gave occasion for healing. It was this very brokenness that gave an opportunity for listening, paying attention, discerning, and responding to what God was saying through the everyday experiences of life. It was in the pain of this tension that my colleagues discovered a new measure of healing and wholeness for their lives and a new vitality and joy in ministry.

Spiritual life is a given. We are created for companionship with God. While we can deny our heart's true home, it does not change the reality of who we are as God's children. Compassion for the hurts of the world is also a part of God's gracious gift of creation of all humankind. But, just as spirituality is learned as well as given, so is compassion and action. We learn the rhythms of spirituality through study, prayer, and practice. And we learn the rhythms of compassion and action through prayer, study, and practice. Therefore, one of the effective ways of bringing healing to this tension or brokenness is to begin to practice a rhythm of life that includes paying attention to the journey inward as well as to the journey outward.

In their book, *Benchmarks of Quality in the Church*, Gustav Rath and Norman Shawchuck declare that "it is the quality of a pastor's relationship to God that determines the quality of a pastor's vision and ministry." Carlo Caretto heard God say to him, "Carlo, old boy, it is not your work that I want, I want you." It does not take one long to realize that if God fully "has us," God also fully has our work. Thus, our prayer and our action become that healthy rhythm of life that leads to fulfillment and fruitfulness in our ministry.

Love of God and love of neighbor are of a piece. They are two threads out of which we daily weave the seamless garment of spirituality. One is first and the other is like it (Matt. 22:37-40). Both of these threads are essential to the Christian life. Both of these threads are also necessary to our joyful and faithful living. Central to God's gracious activity of redemption in the world is the Christian's love of God and neighbor.

In Henry Simmons's book, *In the Footsteps of the Mystics,* this theme has been addressed helpfully by many who have gone before us. What can we learn from their experience?

1. The tension is normal and the place where God meets us.
2. It is possible to live with this wound of tension and still be faithful and fruitful in ministry.
3. Many have been able to fashion a healthy rhythm of prayer, action, and reflection that has led to effective, joyful, and faithful ministry.
4. Our doing can be an occasion for our formation in Christ, for our becoming more fully what we have been created to be.
5. Our being who we are as Christians, inevitably leads us into action in the world.

In every case, those who have gone before us recognized the importance of nurturing the being and the doing parts of our becoming mature Christians. They were skillful in devising occasions, methods, and principles that helped them to be attentive and responsive to God's invitation to become all that they were intended to be.

To follow Jesus as Christian and as Christian minister today is to be led to discover space and time apart for prayer, reflection, and renewal. It is also to be led to redemptive action in the world that God loves. There will always be this "wound of tension" created by the demands of the world and our hunger for God. To recognize this wound is to have discovered the doorway into a vital and renewed ministry and direction for our journey toward Christian maturity.

Many pastors have found that a simple way of life helps them to keep focused on the balance they seek in the ministry. To begin every day with a structure of prayer and reflection can help us to see all of life's activities as occasion for faithful response to God's gracious invitation to companionship. To begin every day with focused attention on God and God's agenda for our lives is inevitably to hear God's voice calling us to rest and reflection and to compassion and action.

Since we are uniquely made and gifted, it is important that each one of us fashion our way of life so as to affirm each of these two important threads of our Christian life and ministry. Before this day apart has ended, take time to listen for God's voice to you. Ask yourself what God is saying to you where you are at this moment in your life's journey. Tell God what you are experiencing in ministry, how it feels, and what you need. It is through such honest prayer and active listening that God's direction comes to us.

Before you leave this place sketch out for yourself a way of life against which you can measure your faithfulness to being and doing. It will give you occasion to note whether or not the desired balance is present in your life and ministry. Use the material in the appendix to guide your efforts.

And do not be surprised at the tension you experience between time required for the demanding ministry that is yours and the time required for quality relationship with God. As the Epistle writer says, "Do not think something strange is happening to you" (1 Peter 4:12-19, AP). Further, I encourage every Christian minister to find a spiritual friend, covenant group, or wise parent in the faith who can help you to listen to and respond faithfully to the voice of God. Be willing to take some new and bold steps, both in the area of contemplation and action. You will discover that learning takes place not only through study and reflection, but through the very act of doing. Invite the Shepherd of your soul to lead and nurture you as you seek to be fully formed in Christ.

SPIRITUAL  READINGS

— PRAYER —

O God of Peace,
    You have taught us not to be anxious in our living.
    Release us from feeling frenzied about our commitments.
    Free us from the burden of our many fears,
        so that we may place our whole trust in your wise care
        and be at peace in the sure knowledge of your love.
    We offer our anxious hearts to you for the healing of faith.
    Through Christ, our living Lord. *Amen.*

—Marjorie J. Thompson

— DAILY CLATTER —

The time of business does not with me differ from the time of prayer; and in the noise and clatter of my kitchen, while several persons are at the same time calling for different things, I possess God in as great tranquility as if I were upon my knees at the blessed sacrament. . . . I made this my business as much all the day long as at the appointed times of prayer; for at all times, every hour, every minute, even in the height of my business, I drove away from my mind everything that was capable of interrupting my thought of God. . . . I found myself changed all at once, and my soul which till that time was in trouble, felt a profound inward peace, as if she were in her center and place of rest.

—Brother Lawrence
The Practice of the Presence of God

THE TENSION BETWEEN DOING AND BEING
— PRAYING IN THE MIDST OF LIFE —

There is a saint of Greece called Maxim, a young man, who went to church one day and heard the reading of the Epistle in which it says that we should pray unceasingly. It struck him in such a way that he thought he could do nothing else than fulfill this commandment. He walked out of the church, went into the neighboring mountains and set out to pray unceasingly. Being a Greek peasant of the fourth century, he knew the Lord's Prayer and some other prayers. So he proceeded, as he tells us, to recite them, again and again and again. Then he felt very well. He was praying, he was with God, he was elated, everything seemed to be so perfect, except that gradually the sun began to go down and it became colder and darker, and as it became darker he began to hear all sorts of worrying sounds—cracking branches under the paws of wild beasts, flashing eyes, sounds of smaller beasts being killed by larger beasts, and so forth. Then he felt that he was really alone, a small, unprotected thing in a world of danger, of death, of murder, and that he had no help if God didn't give it. He no longer continued saying the Lord's Prayer and the Creed; he did exactly what Bartimaeus did, he began to shout, "Lord Jesus Christ, Son of God, have mercy on me." And he shouted like that all the night because the creatures and the flashing eyes didn't give him a chance to go to sleep. Then the morning came and he thought, because all the beasts had gone to sleep, "Now I pray," but by then he felt hungry. He thought he would collect some berries and he started towards a bush, but then he realized that all those flashing eyes and savage paws must be hidden somewhere in the bushes. So he began to make his way very softly and at every step said, "Lord Jesus Christ, save me, help me, help me, save me. O God, help me, protect me," and for every berry he collected he had certainly prayed several times.

Time passed and after many years he met a very old and experienced acetic who asked him how he had learn to pray unceasingly. Maxim said, "I think it's the devil who taught me to pray unceasingly." The other man said, "I think I understand what you mean, but I would like to be sure that I understand you right." Maxim explained how he had gradually become accustomed to all these noises and dangers of the day and night. But then temptations came upon him, temptations of the flesh, temptations of the mind, of the emotions, and later more violent attacks from the devil. After that there was no moment day or night when he did not shout Godwards, saying, "Have mercy, have mercy, help, help, help." Then one day after fourteen years of that, the Lord appeared to him; and the moment the Lord appeared, stillness, peace, serenity came on him. There was no fear left—of darkness or of bushes, no fear of the devil—the Lord had taken over. "By then," Maxim said, "I had learned that unless the Lord himself comes, I am hopelessly and completely helpless. So even when I was serene and peaceful and happy I went on praying 'Lord Jesus Christ, Son of God, have mercy on me'," because he knew that only in the divine mercy was there any peace of heart and peace of mind and stillness of body and rightness of will.

So Maxim learn to pray not in spite of the turmoil, but because of the turmoil, and because the turmoil was a real danger. If we could be aware that we are in much greater turmoil, that the devil is lurking, trying to catch and destroy us, that every human meeting is judgment, is crisis, is a situation in which we are called either to receive Christ or to be Christ's messenger to the person whom we are meeting, if we realized that the whole of life has this intensity of meaning, then we would be able to cry and to pray continuously, and turmoil would be not a hindrance but the very condition which teaches us to pray while we are still too inexperienced to pray from the depth without any prompting, without any incitement into prayer.

When we know nothing about prayer, when we have not prayed at all in our lives or not enough, how can we learn to pray in the conditions of life in which we live? I have experimented on that in a variety of situations: in the years when I was in medical work, five years in the war, in the priesthood and so forth, and it does work. It does work if you are simple enough to do it. It works in this way.

Awake in the morning and the first thing you do, thank God for it, even if you don't feel particularly happy about the day which is to come. "This day which the Lord has made, let us rejoice and be grateful in it." Once you have done this, give yourself time to realize the truth of what you are saying and really mean it—perhaps on the level of deep conviction and not of what one might call exhilaration. And then get up, wash, clean, do whatever else you have to do, and then come to God again. Come to God again with two convictions. The one is that you are God's own and the other is that this day is also God's own, it is absolutely new, absolutely fresh. It has never existed before. To speak in Russian terms, it is like a vast expanse of unsoiled snow. No one has trodden on it yet. It is all virgin and pure in front of you. And now, what comes next? What comes next is that you ask God to bless this day, that everything in it should be blessed and ruled by him. After that you must take it seriously, because very often one says, "O God, bless me," and having got the blessing we act like the prodigal son—we collect all our goods and go to a strange country to lead a riotous life.

This day is blessed by God, it is God's own and now let us go into it.

You walk in this day as God's own messenger; whomever you meet, you meet in God's own way. You are there to be the presence of the Lord God, the presence of Christ, the presence of the Spirit, the presence of the Gospel—this is your function on this particular day. . . . You must be prepared to walk into situations, one after the other, in God's name, to walk as the Son of God has done: in humiliation and humility, in truth and ready to be persecuted and so forth. Usually what we expect when we fulfill God's commandments is to see a marvellous result at once—we read of that at times in the lives of the saints. When, for instance, someone hits us on one cheek, we turn the other one, although we don't expect to be hit at all, but we expect to hear the other person say, "What, such humility"—you get your reward and he gets the salvation of his soul. It does not work that way. You must pay the cost and very often you get hit hard. What matters is that you are prepared for that. As to the day, if you accept that this day was blessed of God, chosen by God . . . then every person you meet is a gift of God, whether it is bitter or sweet, whether you like or dislike it. It is God's own gift to you and if you take it that way, then you can face any situation. . . . You act and pray in one breath, as it were, because all the situations that follow one another require God's blessing. . . .

In this way we can just rest and look at things which are also God's things—trees and buildings—and then after a while we go back to him. If we try to pray continuously, we will be defeated quite soon; but if we choose moments intelligently we can do it.

—Anthony Bloom
Beginning to Pray

— INADVERTENT MINISTRY —

Every minister is a Calvinist come Monday morning. Shuddering to think how little of one's carefully aimed ministry has hit the mark the day before, one feels the truth come thundering home that often the most effective ministry is altogether unplanned, unintentional, even accidental. Were it not for the hope of such inadvertent ministry, many of us would despair altogether.

In 1737 Jonathan Edwards spoke of "the Surprising Work of God at Northampton" and, in the process, penned a classic in the annals of inadvertent ministry. By contrast, I'm exhausted by my own efforts at carefully programmed effectiveness and long to stumble into the serendipitous grace of which he spoke. In those rare moments of unpremeditated ministry when I do happen upon the holy, there is a Zenlike freedom and ease which characterize my best work. It flows without the constant interruption of my ego's trying to imprint itself on all that is accomplished. How to get out of the way of what would exercise itself through me if I let it?

Something of an answer presented itself this past spring at the Fifth Annual St. Louis Storytelling Festival at the Arch. I had been invited to be one of the tellers. Though I used story a great deal in teaching, I'd seldom worked in a performance setting. So while I was excited, I was also terrified. But Laura Simms, a superbly gifted story-teller from New York City, was also at the festival. I told her how frightened I was, saying that I didn't feel like a "real story-teller." She then said something that I'll never forget: "You know, I don't think there *are* any story-tellers. There are only stories and each of us gets to carry one of them for a little while." In that one stroke, she not only greatly eased my fears, but also summarized the whole mystery of ministry. In the final analysis, there aren't any polished and professional manipulators of the Word, there are only stories that seek out their own hearers and tellers, in their own time. One never knows, then, who might be a bearer of the Word. Laura Simms had thus opened for me a way of being a vehicle for the gift without having to pretend mastery over it. She also had given me the perfect conclusion to a story I was to tell the next day.

The story was one whose skeleton I had found in a collection of *Legends of the Hasidim,* by Jerome Mintz (University of Chicago Press, 1968). It's strange how the bones of a story will sometimes leap off the page, demanding to be put into flesh. This story was like that. It was set in Eastern Europe at the end of the 18th century. There in the village of Bobov, in the region of the rich, black earth of Galicia north of the Carpathian Mountains, a rebbe lived and prayed among his small community of poor, Hasidic Jews. One day a couple came to the rebbe to ask him to pray for them, explaining that they had never had a child, though they had waited in patient silence for years. They knew the prayers of the rebbe were able to shake the very gates of heaven itself. So they were jubilant when he said that not only would he pray for them, but he would tell them a story as well. That was better yet!

He spoke of three Hasidim who one year had longed to spend the High Holy Days with the great Lubliner rebbe, Reb Yaakov-Yitzhak of Lublin, also known as the Holy Seer. This fascinating rebbe, blind in one eye but steeped in the wisdom of Talmud and Kabbala, could see, it was said, "from one end of the world to the other." People came to Lublin to study, to meditate, to sit in the shadow of the great seer. Anxious to join this company, the three Jews set out early one fall morning. Without food, without money, they determined to walk all the way to the Polish border and beyond. But after several days without eating, they grew weak with hunger. "Listen," one of the three finally said, "it's no great mitzvah that Jews should die of starvation on their way to see the Holy Seer of Lublin! We've got to do something! According to Torah, anything may be done to save a life." Another suggested that one of them disguise himself as a rebbe. Then whenever they came to a village, people would welcome them warmly, thinking it an honor they should be visited by a rebbe. In this way, at least they'd be fed. None of them wanted to practice deceit, but reluctantly they drew straws and the unfortunate one became the pretending rebbe. A second one dressed up like his gabbai, an assistant working in the house of study; and the third would simply be a Hasid from the community.

On they walked until they came to the next village. There they were greeted with cries of delight: "A rebbe is coming! A rebbe is coming!" They were taken to the inn, and the innkeeper, after seeing to their needs, spoke with great anguish. "Rebbe," he said, "you must pray for my son. He lies dying on his bed at this moment; the doctors say there's no hope. But the Holy One, blessed be His name, may at last respond to your prayers, now that you've come." The "rebbe" looked at his companions to ask what he should do. They motioned him to go with the father. "Don't talk." they said. "Just go with him." There was nothing else to do. Having begun pretending, one had to finish.

That night the three slept restlessly. The next morning the grateful father, hoping the prayer might yet be heard, sent away the rebbe and his retinue, having loaned them a carriage and a matched pair of sable horses for the remainder of their trip. On they went to Lublin, where they spent the days following Rosh Hashana in glorious study and prayer, under the spell of the Lubliner rebbe. With his words the spiced wine of Talmud flowed through their minds and veins. But then came the end of Yom Kippur and the time to return home—back the way they had come, back through the same village once more, back to return the carriage and matched sable pair they had borrowed. The rebbe pretender was especially fearful. His heart was in his throat as he approached the village and saw the innkeeper running toward them, furiously waving his arms in the air. But, to the "rebbe's" joy and relief, the father embraced him, crying, "Rebbe, thank you for your prayers! One hour after you left, my son got out of bed and has been perfectly well ever since! The doctors say it is impossible, but he lives!" The other two Jews looked strangely at the pretending rebbe. Had he really been a rebbe all along, without telling them?

Later he explained that he had gone to the bedside of the child and stood there in silence, as they had told him to do. Then he started to think, "Master of the Universe, this man and his child ought not to be punished because they think I'm a rebbe. What am I? I'm nothing! Just a

97

pretender! After I leave, the child will probably die and the father will be tempted to think that a rebbe can do nothing. So, *Ribbono Shel Olom*, Master of the Universe, not because of me, but because of the man and his faith, can it hurt that the child be healed?" He had done nothing more than that, he said. Strange that such an artless and inadvertent prayer should be heard and answered.

Having finished his story, the rebbe who had been speaking to the couple then said he would pray for them as he had promised. With tired eyes he looked to heaven and, taking upon himself the anguish of every childless couple in the world, he prayed, "Master of the Universe, this man and his wife ought not to be punished because they think I'm a rebbe. What am I? I'm nothing! Just a pretender. We all are pretenders! So, not because of anything that I am, but because of the couple and their patient faith, can it hurt that they be given a child?" The people of the village of Bobov swear that a year later the man and his wife brought their eight-day-old son to the rebbe for *bris*, for circumcision—the son who had been born in answer to a story that was told and an even stranger prayer that was said.

I told this story under the Arch that Sunday morning, moved by the uncalculated ministry of both pretending rebbes. I added a postscript: I suggested that there's a sense in which every story-teller—everyone who ministers, in whatever medium—can and must pray: "Master of the Universe, these people ought not to be punished because they think I'm a story-teller. What am I? I'm nothing. Just a pretender. We *all* are pretenders. So, not because of what I am, but because of the power of the story itself and their faith in it and in You, let them be healed." Such a prayer, I suspect, is one God simply can't resist.

A friend who is both student and teacher to me told me that he does very well at serving as *host*; it's learning to be a *guest* that comes harder for him. He can direct and lead; he can make people feel at home and manage others quite readily. But it's receiving and accepting, the gracious and humble posture of not being in control, that he finds more difficult. That's precisely the dilemma of planned as opposed to inadvertent ministry. Perhaps the problem with most training for ministry today is that it teaches us to be effective hosts, while offering very little about learning to be joyous guests.

Yet being a guest at one's own inadvertent ministry is a graced event, one of the most exultant we may discover. Maybe it happens most often on a Monday, when conscious ministry has been exhausted and we find ourselves seeking once again the back-road villages on the way to Lublin.

—Belden C. Lane
The Christian Century

THE TENSION BETWEEN DOING AND BEING
— LEARNING GOD'S DANCE —

Some fifty years ago Sydney Carter wrote the modern arrangement of an old Shaker hymn called "The Lord of the Dance." It is unusual in that it pictures God as master of the cosmic dance of creation. The One who has danced in the moon and the stars and the sun was also born in Bethlehem to dance on the earth. In his goodness he offers to let us share in his dance, and he will lead us all, wherever we might be.

The imagery here captures perfectly what true Christian life is all about: learning to dance to God's tune. Christian life is not doing our own thing, or dancing our own dance. We are not alone in the dance. It was first learned and danced to perfection by Jesus, who was one with God and in harmony with all of creation. Its varied steps are spelled out in the scriptures. Even better, the essence of this melody is repeated for us over and over again in the Sunday liturgy. Eucharist is the tune of the one who danced even on the Friday when the sun turned black as he hung on the cross. For he is the life that will never, never die. His greatest desire is to live again in us so that the dance may go on.

For years we tended to think of the sacraments as things. Each was thought of in terms of a special grace, which we received from it. Vatican II has reminded us that the sacraments are liturgical actions, not things. *Eucharist*, for example, is an action of the church gathered together, not something done by the priest. If we ever thought of the sacraments as actions of the church previously, it was because they were dispensed in and by the church. However, the *Constitution on the Sacred Liturgy* reminds us that "the full and active participation of all the people is the aim to be considered before all else" (no. 14).

As actions, it is helpful to think of the liturgy as a dance God invites us to join. We are affected by what we do. To speak of the liturgy as a dance is to realize that it is God who pipes the tune, who sets the basic rhythms. For each of us the dance will be different, reflecting the differences in our bodies, our lives, our relationships. This can be a frightening thought for those who prefer a clear-cut pattern, a uniform set of steps that all of us must dance.

However, there is really no fixed form we all must observe. We are not asked to mimic Jesus' steps, although we are to be inspired by his music. We need to let this speak to us and inspire us to dance as Jesus did, filled with his own Spirit. The question is not what Jesus himself might have danced were he alive today. We really don't know. Rather, we need to ask how we might be to people today what Jesus was to people in his own time. This is learning to dance to the same tune that Jesus did, a tune that comes from God. And though its basic rhythms are the same, the steps will differ depending on the circumstances of time and place.

—Paul Bernier
Eucharist: Celebrating Its Rhythms in Our Lives

— *SITTING QUIETLY IN THE SNOW* —

Any serious, daily practice of interior prayer will give some taste of the following experience: You sit in prayer. On the surface there is nothing. Yet, as the noise of your next thought falls away, as you allow the silence to deepen around and within you, you discover that you are on the trackless waters on which Jesus bid Peter to walk in order to be united with him. To use the imagery of Saint John of the Cross, there is a path to walk with "no light except the one that burns in your heart." You set out to find him who calls you out of nothingness to union with himself. You set out knowing that you must find God, yet the first step leaves you lost. An inner wisdom tells you that "to reach him whom you do not know you must go by a way you do not know."

Prayer as described here never touches us as long as it remains on the surface of our lives, as long as it is nothing but one more of the thousand things that must be done. It is only when prayer becomes "the one thing necessary" that real prayer begins. Prayer begins to take on its full dimensions only when we begin to intuit that the subtle nothingness of prayer is everything. Prayer begins when we go to our place of prayer as to a sacred place, when we realize that our own heart is the place where Jacob's ladder touches the earth. . . .

A small green apple cannot ripen in one night by tightening all its muscles, squinting its eyes and tightening its jaw in order to find itself the next morning miraculously large, red, ripe and juicy beside its small green counterparts. Like the birth of a baby or the opening of a rose, the birth of the true self takes place in God's time. We must wait for God, we must be awake; we must trust in his hidden action within us. . . .

A man who, while out walking alone on a bitter cold and starless night, unexpectedly comes upon a large, warm-looking house. Upon approaching the house and pressing his face against the window, he sees himself sleeping comfortably before the fire! Suddenly, he realizes that he is trapped outside his own house. He realizes his life is rich, yet he stands impoverished. He is secure yet he stands on the edge of death. He is fulfilled yet he stands sterile and empty.

Frantically, he begins to pound upon the window, yelling loudly to be let in. But the self inside does not hear and, as he pounds, the glass barrier dividing him from his life only grows thicker and his clenched fists grow numb with pain.

At long last, realizing finally that all efforts of brute force achieve nothing, he sits quietly in the snow overcome by a growing single silent desire, by an unfaltering hope, that he might be one with himself. This desire, though appearing powerless, awakens the self within and with this awakening the glass itself dissolves. The house dissolves and he discovers that he was really at home all along and did not know it. He finds the night to be in fact his light and the bitter cold to be itself a consuming fire of utter joy and fulfillment.

This discovery, is the discovery of the contemplative way. It is a discovery so far beyond our understanding that it calls for the faith of a John the Baptist. John, while in prison, received word from Jesus that, "blessed are they who are not scandalized in me." In effect, John was called upon to realize that losing his head is of itself no cause for alarm. It is just his head. With faith we can lose all, even our head, and by our loss find ourselves richer than kings.

—James Finley
Merton's Palace of Nowhere

— THE PASTOR AS A CHRIST-BEARER —

"Christ-bearer; image of God; symbol of the sacred." Tom kept repeating these ideas to himself as he parked and made his way to the hospital elevator. He thought about all the tasks of ministry—preaching, teaching, counseling, baptizing, conducting funerals, offering the sacrament of the Lord's Supper—could he, in all these functions of ministry, be the bearer of Christ?

Perhaps more pressing, could he be the bearer of Christ to Juanita Jones in room 803, who had learned yesterday that she had an inoperable malignancy?

Tom MacGreggor has been confronted with an issue with which he must come to grips, a calling to re-present Jesus Christ in his life and ministry. This commission to be a Christ-bearer has its source in the heart of the gospel—created in the image of God, re-created by Christ, called by God to be a servant in the church. These roots of pastoral spirituality must ripen into the fruits of Christian ministry.

The symbolic role of the minister as a Christ-bearer introduces a transition from the *being* of the pastor to the pastor's *doing*. Spirituality includes awareness but extends beyond awareness to a lifestyle and a particular form of ministry. At this point we must ask, "How does the spirituality of being a minister express itself in doing ministry?" When a

101

minister claims to be called of God, to be a set-apart person who represents the will of God in Christ, how does this identity affect the practice of ministry?

The pastor as the image of Christ provides an appropriate transition from being to doing because when the minister is the image of the Sacred, the being *is* the doing. The being of the minister in the image of God is doing ministry. This form of being cannot be created or enhanced by the minister's own efforts. It is gift; it is inherent in the fact of the call. Just like a sacrament, the meaning is experienced in the action.

Understanding the minister as the embodiment of the presence of Christ shifts the focus from the minister as an entertainer, therapist, or manager to an ordered of time, a spiritual guide, a leader who seeks to actualize the will of God in concrete actions. This identification centers the minister in Jesus Christ, as one who has been called by God. This designation does not in any way discount the importance of sermons, management, counseling, or social engagement; rather, this perspective grounds these aspects of ministry in the re-presentation of Christ.

—Ben Campbell Johnson
Pastoral Spirituality

Ministers have to be more radical than anyone in living a contemplative life—which means living a life in which we trust that the love we need will be given to us by God. That is essential to the prayer life.

—Henri J. M. Nouwen
Christian Century

First of all, we know that God is the beginning, middle and end of everything good; and it is impossible for us to have faith in anything good or to carry it into effect except in Christ Jesus and the Holy Spirit.

—St. Nikodimos

QUAKER SPIRITUALITY

One of the most impressive twentieth-century American mystics, Thomas R. Kelly (1893–1941), drew on Quaker traditions to write the following:

Under the silent, watchful eye of the Holy One we are all standing, whether we know it or not. And in that center, in that holy Abyss where the Eternal dwells at the base of our being, our programs, our gifts to Him, our offerings of duties performed are again and again revised in their values. Many of the things we are doing seem so important to us. We haven't been able to say No to them, because they seem so important. But if we *center down*, as the old phrase goes, and live in that holy Silence which is dearer than life, and take our life program into the silent places of the heart, with complete openness, ready to do, ready to renounce according to His leading, then many of the things we are doing lose their vitality for us. I should like to testify to this, as a personal experience, graciously given. There is a reevaluation of much that we do or try to do, which is *done for us*, and we know what to do and what to let alone.

. . . Kelly's conviction that we are all standing under the silent, watchful eye of the Holy One is not peculiar to him or the Quakers. Many others drawn to God have realized that, if God truly is what we say about God, every moment unfolds before him, no thought or desire escapes his knowing. Kelly, though, is more direct than most in making the constant presence of God his spiritual center. Alternately, he calls it a holy abyss. Our center is not ourselves. Something awesome yawns in our depths. The eternal, the divine mystery itself, dwells at the foundations of our being, is the foundation of our being.

Once again, the insight is not novel. But the language is beginning to be. For the language brims with personal experience. Kelly is not offering a treatise so much as a testimony. He has experienced the foundation of his being. The eternal has made itself known. The divine abyss has become his own yawning center. And, in consequence, everything in his life has changed. Nothing ordinary is important now, and yet everything ordinary is important. Everything is different, yet many things seem for the first time to be themselves. A lovely paradox rivets his interest.

In this paassage, the things of greatest interest to Kelly the preacher are personal projects. What good people would do for God, offer to God, carry out as holy duties fall into a new pattern when the presence of God becomes habitual. They do not go away. We do not call them wrong or irrelevant. But we do realize that they are means, rather than ends. We do rethink the importance they have gained in our psyches, the large degree to which we have come to define ourselves through them. No longer can our charities, our books, even our intercessory prayers rise up as imperative. They have no intrinsic urgency. All their rightful urgency comes from God's obliging us to them.

Indeed, what keeps this line of thought from spiritual platitude is the source of the rearrangement Thomas Kelly is struggling to describe. He does not sit down with a notebook to tally his accounts. He is not giving us a little lesson in moral reform. He is reporting, with considerable amazement, how his own psyche, his own self, was rearranged. God happened to him. God became real. In consequence, his life as a philosophy professor, a husband and father, a leading light of Pennsylvania Quakerism in the 1930s—all this changed dramatically, at least on the inside.

To outward appearances, Kelly was simply more joyous than he had previously been. The good humor that his friends had long loved simply shone brighter. But a few intimate friends learned that great things had happened to him interiorly. He now felt completely surrendered to God and guided by a divine light.

When he tries to describe in writing, for the benefit of others, the easing of strain that his experience of God has produced, Kelly notes that it has taken away most of his compulsiveness. He no longer feels a victim of American activism. He can do his best but not feel he has to overcommit himself—go beyond his strength, hoist every good work that comes his way. He is less important than he used to think. The projects that come his way are less pressing. Any one of them may be good in itself, but few are imperative. Indeed, the new imperative in his life is not doing but being. The new treasure is not speech but silence. . . .

To finish with Kelly, the final point to gloss is his testimony that the rearrangement of affairs that he has experienced more happened to him than came from his own doing. Things he previously considered imperative lost their vitality, their life-or-death character, because he underwent a divine action that reentered his conscious being. He now knows what to do, and what to let alone, because now the vital principle directing his discernment is not his own intelligence and will but the divine presence. A new, right order has come to prevail in his soul. He knows, not just notionally but really, that God is everything and he is nothing. He knows, with bite and savor, that God can raise up children of Abraham from inert stones. Like Socrates he is ruled by an inner voice warning him off courses of action, even courses of thought, that would take him into disorder. Unlike Socrates, he feels positive lurings as well, and he thinks of his inner voice or light as the presence of the personal Creator, the Lord of Hosts. . . .

We might say, then, that the two imperatives of Quaker spirituality merge into one. The overarching need is to become identified with God, who is love. Better, the overarching need is to dispose oneself to God's granting such an identification. Like all genuine mystics, Kelly reports that the crux of union with God is more passive than active. God is the one who gives this union. God is the one who clarifies the social concerns that the union makes imperative. Becoming identified with God, through God's doing, creates the discernment of what is truly important and what is merely a matter of human desire. Becoming identified with God brings about the change of mind and heart, the overturning of prior worldly assumptions, necessary for effective Christian action. The world looks very different, when God is supplying the horizon. The real, experiential assumption of the mind of Christ reveals that one is in the midst of a new creation.

Identification with God, so that loving God is one's pearl of great price, makes for a radical contemplation and a radical action. At the roots of one's being, both what is so and what is to be done seem newly fashioned. Kelly and others can talk on and on, but until those they address have been taken over by the divine spirit, their words will not carry to the heart. Only God can make people understand the gospel. Only God can make "God" alive, more intimate to us than we are to ourselves, the very font of reality.

Our part is to want such a grace, to crave such a transformation. We cannot bring it about, but we can desire it. Logically, such a desire might seem to conflict with Jesus' prayer that his Father's will be done, not his own. In practice, there is no conflict. What we desire, when we are ardent for God, has to become the hallowing of God's name, the coming of God's kingdom, the doing of God's will. As we mature, our passion becomes that God increase and we decrease. Only God is holy, mighty, immortal. We are but creatures of a day, but grass. The grass withers, the flowers fade. Only the Word of the Lord endures.

The Word of God, the wisdom that identification with God imprints in our souls, is that God is love and so infinitely creative. There are no dead ends in God. That is why union with God is such a boost to political hope. As I write, Israelis and Arabs sit down in Madrid to negotiate peace in the Middle East. The majority of commentators are delighted that these bitter foes are meeting but pessimistic about any significant results. The American Friends Service Committee cannot be pessimistic. For well over a decade, it has urged dialogue and reconciliation. There can be no impossibilities with God. Especially in the spiritual order, the divine creativity makes freedom the sovereign rule. Who could have predicted the spiritual victories in Eastern Europe and the Soviet Union that led to the demise of inhuman Communist regimes? Only those who, like the most astute Friends, had been formed by silence to disregard human cynicism and reckon the will of God the most significant factor in human affairs.

—John Carmody
Spiritual Life

— A RELEVANT QUESTION —

My son-in-law, Alan Jones, told me a story of a Hassidic rabbi, renowned for his piety. He was unexpectedly confronted one day by one of his devoted youthful disciples. In a burst of feeling, the young disciple exclaimed, "My master, I love you!" The ancient teacher looked up from his books and asked his fervent disciple, "Do you know what hurts me, my son?"

The young man was puzzled. Composing himself, he stuttered, "I don't understand your question, Rabbi. I am trying to tell you how much you mean to me, and you confuse me with irrelevant questions."

"My question is neither confusing nor irrelevant," rejoined the rabbi, "for if you do not know what hurts me, how can you truly love me?"

—Madeleine L'Engle
Walking on Water

— FIRST THINGS —

For too long we have thought of the Christian life as essentially either involvement in political, economic, social concerns that wear us out and result in depression or activity which keeps the church intact and doctrinally pure. Our primary orientation cannot be to an institution or some great cause or even other people, but first and forever to God. Unless our identity is hid in God we will never know who we are or what we are to do. Our first act must be prayer, *Oratio*. To be human is to pray, to meditate both day and night on the love and activity of God. We are called to be continuously formed and transformed by the thought of God within us. Prayer is a disciplined dedication to paying attention. Without the singleminded attentiveness of prayer we will rarely hear anything worth repeating or catch a vision worth asking anyone else to gaze upon.

Too many of us are thinking these days as the world thinks because we do not begin our thinking by thinking about God. Only by paying attention to God will we experience the ecstasy that leads to wisdom. Prayer is that work, that disciplined attentiveness, that bold losing of oneself, that openness to divine leading which defines the everyday spiritual life of every human being. We are called to work and pray. But if we don't pray, if we don't pay close attention to God, our work becomes drudgery rather than vocation, meaningless rounds of activities rather than meaningful human life, even our actions on behalf of social justice become self-righteous and self-serving rather than a radical witness to true human life.

Prayer is at the heart of the Christian life. Prayer is communion with God, a personal response to God's presence.

—John H. Westerhoff III and John D. Eusden
The Spiritual Life: Learning East and West

— LOVE OF GOD AND NEIGHBOR —

"What is the relationship between the love of God and the love of neighbor?" In what precise ways are the love of God and the love of neighbor bound together? Are they inextricably interwoven? Can they be separated? Is one of more importance than the other? Is one prior to the other? Is one possible without the other? Are they of different "orders"— that is, does one love the neighbor directly and God only indirectly?

The question may also be understood to inquire about God's love for the neighbor as well as our love for the neighbor. Do we discover who is our neighbor by asking who it is that God loves? Does God's love for our neighbor put demands on us? Who is our neighbor? Are family and friends *more* our neighbor than those at a distance?

As with the other questions, your interpretation of the question as well as your response is of great importance. In your life you have sorted out your answer in action and words; and your answer reflects your understanding of the question and its importance for the spiritual life. Try now to be as full as you can in your answer to the question: "What is the relationship between the love of God and the love of neighbor?" Think back over your life—has your answer always been the same as it is today? What are the turning points in your understanding of this question? How does it color your relationship to family and friends, to strangers and enemies? Take time to answer the question as fully as you can; cherish your own answers and your own starting points in the conversation.

—Henry C. Simmons
In the Footsteps of the Mystics

— WITHOUT CONTEMPLATION THE PEOPLE PERISH —

For most Christians, contemplation is an awesome word. It conjures up a Paul of Tarsus "caught up to the third heaven" (2 Cor. 12:2), a Teresa of Avila with a vision of "the sorely wounded Christ," Ignatius Loyola seeing or feeling "the Being of the Most Holy Trinity," Lao Tzu apprehending the spiritual essence of Tao. Here I want to speak of a contemplation that is open to all who believe, who love. What is it and how do you get that way?

107

. This is the contemplation that Carmelite William McNamara once called "experiential awareness of reality," a way of entering into immediate communion with the real. "You can study things, but unless you enter into this intuitive communion with them you can only know *about* them, you don't *know* them. To take a long loving look at something—a child, a glass of wine, a beautiful meal—this is a natural act of contemplation, of loving admiration."

Never have I heard contemplation more excitingly described: a long loving look at the real. Each word is crucial. The *real* is not simply some far-off, abstract, intangible God-in-the-sky. Reality is pulsing people, fire and ice, a gentle doe streaking through the forest, the sun setting over the Rockies. Reality is a ruddy glass of Burgundy, Beethoven's "Ode to Joy," a child lapping a chocolate ice-cream cone, a striding woman with wind-blown hair. Reality is the risen Christ with the glorified wounds of his passion. Paradoxically, what alone is excluded from contemplation is abstraction. What I contemplate is always what is most real: what philosophers call the concrete singular.

This real I *look* at. I do not analyze it or argue it, describe or define it; I am one with it. Lounging by a stream, I do not exclaim "Ah H_2O!" I let the water trickle gently through my fingers. I do not theologize about the redemptive significance of Calvary; I link a pierced hand to mine. And it is my whole person that responds to the real. Not only mind, but eyes and ears, smelling and touching and tasting, emotion and passion of which a dehumanizing Anglo-Saxon legacy has made us ashamed. Little wonder that noted theater critic Walter Kerr compared contemplation to falling in love. Not simply knowing another's height, weight, coloring, ancestry, I.Q., acquired habits; rather, "the single, simple vibration that gives us such joy in the meeting of eyes or the lucky conjunction of interchanged words. Something private and singular and uniquely itself is touched—and known in the touching."

This look is a *long* look. For many Americans, time is a stop watch, time is money, life is a race against time. To contemplate is to rest—to rest in the real. Not lifelessly or languidly, not sluggishly or inertly. My entire being is alive, incredibly responsive, vibrating to every throb of the real. For once, time is irrelevant. You do not time the New York Philharmonic, clock the Last Supper.

But this long look must be a *loving* look. It is not a fixed stare, not the long look of a Judas. It demands that the real captivate me, at times delight me. Tchaikovsky's *Swan Lake Ballet* or Lobster Cardinal, the grace of God's swans or the compassion in the eyes of Christ—whatever or whoever the real, contemplation calls forth love, oneness with the other. For contemplation is not study. To contemplate is to be in love.

True, contemplation does not always summon up delight. The real includes sin and war, poverty and race, illness and death. The real is AIDS and abortion, apartheid and MS, bloated bellies and stunted minds, respirators and last gasps. But even here the real I contemplate must end in compassion, and compassion that mimics Christ is a synonym for love.

From such contemplation comes communion. I mean the discovery of the Holy in deep, thoughtful encounters—with God's creation, God's people, God's self—where love is proven by sacrifice, the wild exchange of all for another, for the Other. Thus is fashioned what the second-century bishop Irenaeus called "God's glory—man/woman alive!"

But how realize this capacity for contemplation? Several swift suggestions.

First, *some sort of desert experience*. Not necessarily the physical desert that runs through the Bible, through salvation history, through the desert fathers. Rather that the process can best be initiated by an experience that brings you face to face with solitude, with vastness, even with powers of life and death beyond your control—where the values of life are presented in clear, stark terms. An experience that (in Fr. McNamara's rhetoric) evokes your capacity for initiative, exploration, evaluation; interrupts your ordinary pattern of life; intercepts routine piety. You know yourself, not a statistically polled image of yourself. You know God, not abstractions about God, not even a theology of God, but the much more mysterious and mighty God of theology.

Second, *develop a feeling for festivity*. Festivity, as Josef Pieper noted, resides in activity that is meaningful in itself—not tied to goals. It calls for renunciation: you must take usable time and withdraw it from utility —and this out of love, whose expression is joy. Festivity is a yes to the world, to the reality of things, to the existence of woman and man, to the world's Creator.

A third suggestion, intimately allied to festivity: *a sense of play*. Not "fooling around"; rather what poet Francis Thompson meant when, in his essay on Shelley, he likened the poet's gifts to a child's faculty of make-believe, but raised to the nth power. It demands a sense of wonder that many of us lose as we grow older, get blasé and worldly-wise and sophisticated, believe that everything can be explained. No, let your imagination loose to play with ideas—what it means to be alive, to be in love, to hope even in this valley of darkness.

Fourth, *don't try to possess the object of your delight*, whether divine or human, imprisoned marble or free-flowing rivulet. Here a paragraph from Walter Kerr that has influenced my living far beyond my ability to describe:

To regain some delight in ourselves and in our world, we are forced to abandon, or rather to reverse, an adage. A bird in the hand is not worth two in the bush—unless one is an ornithologist, the curator of the Museum of Natural History, or one of those Italian vendors who supply restaurants with larks. A bird in the hand is no longer a bird at all; it is a specimen; it may be dinner. Birds are birds only when they are in the bush or on the wing; their worth as birds can be known only at a discreet and generous distance.

Fifth, *make friends with remarkable men and women* who have themselves looked long and lovingly at the real. I mean biblical figures like Abraham and Mary; martyrs like Ignatius of Antioch and Martin Luther King; uncanonized women of vision like Dorothy Day, Mother Teresa and Anne Morrow Lindbergh. I mean Lao Tzu doing everything through being, and Abraham Joshua Heschel doing everything through worship; philosophers like Jacques Maritain, insisting that the culmination of knowledge is not conceptual but experiential: man/woman "feels" God. I mean Mr. Blue, Myles Connolly's New York "mystic" who flew kites and exulted in brass bands; short-story writer Flannery O'Connor, dead of lupus at 39, with her mature acceptance of limitation, with so much Christlife in her frail frame—grace on crutches. I mean Thomas Merton, always the contemplative but moving from renunciation to involvement, making contact with Hindu and Buddhist and Sufi, protesting Vietnam and violence, racial injustice and nuclear war. Touch men and women like those, and you will touch the stars, will touch God.

The point of all this? These men and women are not solitaries. Not neurotic escapists. Few of them fled the world, even when they removed to a discreet distance. They are contemplatives in action, flesh and blood in a world of grime and grit—unique, however, because each has smashed through boundaries and stretched human limits to the walls of infinity.

The world is athirst for men and women who know God and love God; for only such can give to today's paradoxical world the witness to a living God that this age demands. My personal failing is to me agonizingly apparent: at times I do not come through as a man who looks long and lovingly at the real. The consequence? Some men and women who touch me do not thrill to the touch, and so they abide in their loneliness, continue to experience the absence of God.

Without contemplation the people perish.

— Walter J. Burghardt, S. J.
Church

The Tension Between Doing and Being
— RAGMAN —

I saw a strange sight. I stumbled upon a story most strange, like nothing my life, my street sense, my sly tongue had ever prepared me for.

Hush, child. Hush, now, and I will tell it to you.

Even before the dawn one Friday morning I noticed a young man, handsome and strong, walking the alleys of our City. He was pulling an old cart filled with clothes both bright and new, and he was calling in a clear, tenor voice: "Rags!" Ah, the air was foul and the first light filthy to be crossed by such sweet music.

"Rags! New rags for old! I take your tired rags! Rags!"

"Now, this is a wonder," I thought to myself, for the man stood six-feet-four, and his arms were like tree limbs, hard and muscular, and his eyes flashed intelligence. Could he find no better job than this, to be a ragman in the inner city?

I followed him. My curiosity drove me. And I wasn't disappointed.

Soon the Ragman saw a woman sitting on her back porch. She was sobbing into a handkerchief, sighing, and shedding a thousand tears. Her knees and elbows made a sad X. Her shoulders shook. Her heart was breaking.

The Ragman stopped his cart. Quietly, he walked to the woman, stepping round tin cans, dead toys, and Pampers.

"Give me your rag," he said so gently, "and I'll give you another."

He slipped the handkerchief from her eyes. She looked up, and he laid across her palm a linen cloth so clean and new that it shined. She blinked from the gift to the giver.

Then, as he began to pull his cart again, the Ragman did a strange thing: he put her stained handkerchief to his own face; and then *he* began to weep, to sob as grievously as she had done, his shoulders shaking. Yet she was left without a tear.

"This *is* a wonder," I breathed to myself, and I followed the sobbing Ragman like a child who cannot turn away from mystery.

"Rags! Rags! New rags for old!"

In a little while, when the sky showed grey behind the rooftops and I could see the shredded curtains hanging out black windows, the Ragman came upon a girl whose head was wrapped in a bandage, whose eyes were empty. Blood soaked her bandage. A single line of blood ran down her cheek.

Now the tall Ragman looked upon this child with pity, and he drew a lovely yellow bonnet from his cart.

"Give me your rag," he said, tracing his own line on her cheek, "and I'll give you mine."

111

The child could only gaze at him while he loosened the bandage, removed it, and tied it to his own head. The bonnet he set on hers. And I gasped at what I saw: for with the bandage went the wound! Against his brow it ran a darker, more substantial blood—his own!

"Rags! Rags! I take old rags!" cried the sobbing, bleeding, strong, intelligent Ragman.

The sun hurt both the sky, now, and my eyes; the Ragman seemed more and more to hurry.

"Are you going to work?" he asked a man who leaned against a telephone pole. The man shook his head.

The Ragman pressed him: "Do you have a job?"

"Are you crazy?" sneered the other. He pulled away from the pole, revealing the right sleeve of his jacket—flat, the cuff stuffed into the pocket. He had no arm.

"So," said the Ragman. "Give me your jacket, and I'll give you mine."

Such quiet authority in his voice!

The one-armed man took off his jacket. So did the Ragman—and I trembled at what I saw: for the Ragman's arm stayed in its sleeve, and when the other put it on he had two good arms, thick as tree limbs; but the Ragman had only one.

"Go to work," he said.

After that he found a drunk, lying unconscious beneath an army blanket, an old man, hunched, wizened, and sick. He took that blanket and wrapped it round himself, but for the drunk he left new clothes.

And now I had to run to keep up with the Ragman. Though he was weeping uncontrollably, and bleeding freely at the forehead, pulling his cart with one arm, stumbling for drunkenness, falling again and again, exhausted, old, old, and sick, yet he went with terrible speed. On spider's legs he skittered through the alleys of the City, this mile and the next, until he came to its limits, and then he rushed beyond.

I wept to see the change in this man. I hurt to see his sorrow. And yet I needed to see where he was going in such haste, perhaps to know what drove him so.

The little old Ragman—he came to a landfill. He came to the garbage pits. And then I wanted to help him in what he did, but I hung back, hiding. He climbed a hill. With tormented labor he cleared a little space on that hill. Then he sighed. He lay down. He pillowed his head on a handkerchief and a jacket. He covered his bones with an army blanket. And he died.

Oh, how I cried to witness that death! I slumped in a junked car and wailed and mourned as one who has no hope—because I had come to love the Ragman. Every other face had faded in the wonder of this man, and I cherished him; but he died. I sobbed myself to sleep.

I did not know—how could I know?—that I slept through Friday night and Saturday and its night, too.

But then, on Sunday morning, I was awakened by a violence.

Light—pure, hard, demanding light—slammed against my sour face, and I blinked, and I looked, and I saw the last and the first wonder of all. There was the Ragman, folding the blanket more carefully, a scar on his forehead, but alive! And, besides that, healthy! There was no sign of sorrow nor of age, and all the rags that he had gathered shined for cleanliness.

Well, then I lowered my head and, trembling for all that I had seen, I myself walked up to the Ragman. I told him my name with shame, for I was a sorry figure next to him. Then I took off all my clothes in that place, and I said to him with dear yearning in my voice: "Dress me."

He dressed me. My Lord, he put new rags on me, and I am a wonder beside him. The Ragman, the Ragman, the Christ!

—Walter Wanergin, Jr.
The Ragman

— THE BREAD OF ANXIOUS TOIL —

The fourteen-hour workday is a perfect metaphor for a way of life so ingrained in our culture that it has virtually become a status symbol. It is as if the busier we are, the more important we must be. I wonder how many of us feel that our lives are justified only if we are continually occupied, flying from one activity to another, from one urgent task to the next. Our cultural values urge us toward a perverse pride in being overextended. If work is good, more work must be better! Isn't it how much we accomplish that gives us our worth? If we believe this, we can keep ourselves near the borders of exhaustion in the name of productivity, commitment, and responsibility. We can even do it in the name of God's "will!"

The second verse of Psalm 127 is quite challenging: "It is vain that you rise up early and go late to rest, eating the bread of anxious toil; for God gives to his beloved, even while they sleep." (AP)

Within this world, work is a necessity, and within the church, active service is an expression of our call. The problem is not work or service. The problem is the pervasive anxiety that we have too much to accomplish in too little time; the worry that what we do will be inadequate, unappreciated, not thought "good enough." It is inner turmoil, felt in the rush and pressure of conflicting concerns, that does us violence.

"It is vain that you rise up early and go late to rest, eating the bread of anxious toil." The bread of anxious toil—isn't that a choice description of what we *try* to sustain ourselves with? We can literally fill ourselves with it, day after day, gulping it down in guilty haste. It is not the toil, but the anxiety that distorts God's glory in our lives. God's goodness and love are obscured by anxiety; anxiety refuses to believe that the Lord "gives to his beloved, even as they sleep." Isn't that a lovely description of pure grace—unearned and unearnable? God delights in children who trust—trust enough to rest in peace, knowing they are embraced by divine care. . . .

In our rapidly changing society, we are especially obsessed with what lies ahead. Why else would we expend so much energy forecasting the economy like weather? Why is much of American religious culture fixated on the Book of Revelation? Why do mainline church leaders try so hard to predict the future of our denominations? We want to know outcomes in advance. Why? Is it not so that we can be as much in control as possible?

Our anxiety about tomorrow seems to be connected to a rather astounding conviction that we could handle things better than God, given half a chance. Maybe that's why some of us take chances wherever we can find them. We keep trying to occupy the driver's seat in this universe. But the seat is just too big for us. So our need for control turns around to terrify and enslave us. It is very stressful to have to be in control of everything! . . .

I hope we'll catch on to the idea that "the bread of anxious toil" is not so necessary as we imagine it to be. Certainly it is no source of sustenance! It is a bitter food, draining away courage, dissipating our energy, sapping away joy and gratitude, and leaving us brooding and exhausted. The bread of anxious toil is truly miserable fare!

Thank God there is another kind of bread—an antidote to the slow poison of anxiety. There is a bread that nourishes us to the core. It refreshes the spirit, calms the mind, heals us, body and soul. Even in the midst of trying circumstances, it offers love strong enough to cast out fear, inspire trust, restore joy, bring peace. This is the Bread of Life, Christ, our God incarnate: "O taste and see that the Lord is good; blessed are all who trust in Him." (Ps. 34:8) To taste the Bread of Life is to know quiet confidence in the midst of frantic activity and confusion.

—Marjorie J. Thompson

— BEATITUDE —

Joyful is she who sets her heart upon God; anxiety
    has no power over her.
To him who discovers freedom in Yahweh will be
    granted strength and serenity; day after day he
    will grow in wisdom.
Favor and blessing is lavished upon the ones who
    discern Ultimate Mystery in the fabric of creation;
    these are the pure in heart.
Evil will not prevail over him who perceives holiness in
    a grasshopper. She will flourish who beholds
    God's Spirit in a disabled child.

But those who dishonor the Almighty, those who
    divest creation of its dignity, will find themselves
    broken apart.
The cyclone of divine judgment shall visit those who
    hurl violence into the midst of innocent lives; the
    empires of those who exploit human suffering will
    be demolished.

The saints are those who adhere to God, and only
    God; their obedience gives birth to ceaseless
    vitality and an incorruptible spirit!
They are like spacewalkers, unfettered by gravity;
    weightless and free, they move through a region
    of unexplored mystery!
To them, the way of Yahweh resounds with confidence
    and awe; they celebrate the incarnation of God's
    justice.
Their joy comes from caring for the downtrodden,
    their fulfillment from reaching out to the
    heartbroken and to the weary.

Those who reject the Preserver of Life are haunted by
    murderous dreams and elusive hopes. But Yahweh
    lifts the burdens of those whose hearts and minds are pure.
The children of the Holy One are adorned with
    becoming; by the joyous embrace of eternal life
    they are cradled.

—Martin Bell
Street Singing and Preaching

RETREAT  PATTERN

Prayer for Guidance

O God of Mercy, make yourself known to me in these hours of retreat. Illumine and remove from my life those sins and distractions that prevent me from being attentive and faithful. Grant to me in this time apart faith, wisdom, and courage to see and rejoice in your promises for my future. *Amen.*

Silent Listening

Scripture Reading

Jeremiah 1:1-10; Romans 12:1-21; 2 Corinthians 4:1-18; Philippians 2:1-18; John 13:1-20; Mark 9:33-37

What are these scripture passages saying to you today?
How does each passage offer insight or direction for your ministry?

Spiritual Reading

Reflection

Mealtime, Rest, Recreation

Journaling

Prayer

Further Spiritual Reading, Reflection, Journaling, Prayer

Eucharist

Response: Thanksgiving, Offerings, Covenant

Returning to the World

Refer to the appendix for suggestions or design your own plan for faithful living. Be sure to provide for time and space to give attention to your relationship with God.

Closing Prayer

Thank you, loving God, for this time of awakening and renewal. By your grace keep me sensitive to your voice of guidance, assurance, comfort, and hope. Help me to see and rejoice in the future you have in store for me. I offer my prayer in the name of the One who knew the cost and the joy of faithfulness. *Amen.*

5.
DO I HAVE A FUTURE IN THE CHURCH?

N ow and then the question was bold and direct. More often, the question was found beneath the surface of other questions and broke through that surface only occasionally when there was unusual openness and honesty. And yet, it is an appropriate question for Christian ministers. It is a question that goes to the heart of Christian discipleship and Christian ministry. Do I have a future in the church? It is a question that should be explored because there is an appropriate response.

For too long we have pretended that the question does not exist. There is ample denial of the fact that pastors have ambitions, desires, and dreams for the future. Frequently we submerge the tension between the call of Jesus Christ to faithful ministry and the call of our culture and of our own will to survive at all costs. We become immersed in the activity of a parish, the politics of a denominational system, the needs of a community, and the concerns of the persons under our care, to the extent that we forget even the most profound questions of our own calling.

But in our reflective moments we hear the questions of our own hearts. If I lose my life for Jesus Christ and the gospel, will I find it? Or, if I lose my life for Jesus Christ and the gospel, will it make any difference? If I follow the way of the cross, will I be seen as some fool who has failed? If I do not scramble for upward mobility and career achievement, will I sacrifice not only my own life, but the life of my family? Can one be an effective minister in contemporary society without grabbing at every opportunity for advancement in the sight of peers and the world? These questions live just beneath the surface and often direct our response to ministry opportunities, conversations with our peers, and response to those we believe have some influence on our destiny.

Robert Schnase, in his book *Ambition in Ministry,* brings unusual clarity to what he calls "the forbidden passion of clergy." He acknowledges the positive and negative attributes of ambition in pastors. He points out the "crippling ambivalence about ambition in the church." The church seems to be relatively clear that mediocrity is no virtue. There seems to be consensus that excellence is a valued attribute for ministry at every level. And yet, when we stand before the One who "emptied himself, took the form of a slave, was found in human form, humbled himself, and became obedient to death on a cross" (Phil. 2:7-8), we recognize that the categories for excellence, for success and failure, that are often used to measure ministry are entirely inadequate.

Writing in *Sojourners* magazine (August, 1981), Henri Nouwen made a significant contribution to the understanding of Christian ministry around the concept of downward mobility.

> Our vocation is to follow Christ on his downward path and become witnesses to God's compassion in the concreteness of our time and place. Our temptation is to let needs for success, visibility, and influence dominate our thoughts, words, and actions to such an extent that we are trapped in the destructive spiral of upward mobility and thus lose our vocation. It is this lifelong tension between vocation and temptation that presents us with the necessity of formation. Precisely because the downward mobility of the way of the cross cannot depend on our spontaneous responses, we are faced with the question, "How do we reach conformity to the mind and heart of the self-emptying Christ?"

Nouwen has correctly identified the tension between the model that Jesus Christ lived out and most contemporary models of "successful ministry." The "self-emptied heart" is what Jesus demonstrated so well and what we have so much difficulty demonstrating. We have difficulty because it is hard to do, because we have so little help from peers or institution, and because it requires a lifetime of attention.

But Nouwen also suggests a way out of this dilemma. He calls us to discipline, but not the discipline of athletics or academics in which new fitness or new knowledge is achieved. "The discipline of the Christian disciple is not to master anything, but rather to be mastered by the Spirit. True Christian discipline is the human effort to create space in which the Spirit of Christ can transform us into his image."

While these words were addressed to both laity and clergy, they are especially appropriate as we consider our call to representative ministry. Pastors are representatives of Christ. The church has recognized us and set us aside for this representative ministry. We live out our calling in every aspect of our lives and especially through the ministries of Word, sacrament, and order. Our responsibility to teach, preach, and to lead those under our care in faithful discipleship, following the One who came "not to be served but to serve, and to give his life as a ransom for many," requires an extra measure of God's grace for each of us.

There are those wonderful examples in every denomination of persons who have taken very seriously the "self-emptying" style of ministry upon themselves. Some of these shepherds have for years practiced ministry in unknown places with unusual commitment and skill. Some of them knew intuitively this was the way to follow Jesus Christ. Others found the way through careful search, learning from failure and the consistent practice of a disciplined spiritual life. But each of them understands a truth about ministry shared by the pastor of Bethel Evangelical Church in Detroit in 1915. With only twenty congregants, pastor and theologian Reinhold Niebuhr did not consider his ministry a failure. He knew it was not where he was but who he was and what he permitted God to do through him that really mattered.

My leisure reading as I write these pages is *The Diary of a Country Priest* by Georges Bernanos. First published in 1937, this novel still has much to teach us. Among the lessons to be learned is the capacity to see every place as an opportunity for faithful ministry. Hidden in all of our questions about the future is the seed of destruction of faithful ministry today. As long as we keep looking at the horizon for our ministry we run the risk of stumbling over the opportunities for ministry that are all around us where we are. In careful observation of those who have demonstrated the capacity for faithful ministry characterized by a self-emptied heart and a life formed into the image of Christ, I have noted a consistent pattern in each of their lives. Their lives are marked with an unusual trust that permits them to act justly, love tenderly, and walk humbly with God (Mic. 6:8).

In every case there is simple trust in God. The words may be different but the theme is the same. God will provide. God's grace is adequate. God will not forsake or abandon God's people. It is this bone-deep trust in God that permits these pastors to live above political intrigue, peer pressure, and disappointment in a congregation's slow response to the gospel. Their preaching, teaching, and daily life in the parish inspires hope and confidence in those who have opportunity to observe their ministry.

Not only is there a common theme of trust in God, but there is a common theme of trust in other persons and in the institutional church. These men and women are certainly not naive about the failures of humankind and the effect this has had on the institutional church. They are not blind to the church's shortcomings, but they know that their ministry is not determined by or dependent upon the behavior of other persons or of the church. Believing that the context for their ministry is larger than church and culture, they are not unduly influenced by either. Believing that God is the context of their ministry, there is awareness that every experience and event of life passes through the hands of God before it comes to them. This informed trust in God, others, and the institution saves them from cynicism, anger, jealousy, and discouragement.

Trust in themselves is another quality that marks the lives of these faithful pastors. They do not "think more highly of themselves" than they should. They do, however, reflect a calm confidence as those who know they have been chosen in love "before the foundation of the world" (Eph. 1:4). Because of their confidence in the Christ within they are able to trust themselves and their ministry. It gives them the courage, boldness, and faith to attempt creative ministry wherever they find themselves. They have learned that trust in God, others, and themselves gives them peace and strength and often saves them from disappointment and disillusionment.

Dietrich Bonhoeffer says that "to deny oneself is to be aware only of Christ and no more of self. To see only him who goes before and no more the road which is too hard for us." To endure the cross is the way of ministry. It is not a road too hard for us because we are companioned by the living Christ and given strength by the power of the Holy Spirit. Obedience to this call to the "self-emptied heart" is never the result of our own power. It is always the result of God's gracious offer to walk with us and God's gracious acts to assist us even when we are unaware of God's presence and power in our lives.

Do you have a future in the church? Of course, but it may not be the future you envision, with upward mobility and acclaim by church and the world. It may be a future marked by a transparent faith in God and a relentless commitment to Jesus Christ. It may be a future without the rewards that are often listed as signs of success.

However, if your future and mine are marked by even the slightest reflection of the life of Christ within who we are, what we do, and how we do ministry, we will have discovered the rewards of a "self-emptied heart." For a heart emptied of self provides space and hospitality to the Christ who seeks to dwell within, and that is reward enough for a lifetime of ministry.

There are those who have discovered the truth of the words of Jesus, to lose one's life is to find it. They live in a new reality, a world that, in spite of evidence to the contrary, is still a place where the radical ways of discipleship can be taught and practiced. They have learned that it is possible to lose one's life and find it as pastor in our contemporary world.

SPIRITUAL  READINGS

— ALWAYS EXCELLING —

The pastor's sudden death surprised us all. Even though he was edging toward retirement, he had seemed too young for this moment. A host of lay people and a gallery of pastors gathered to hear a succession of kindred clergy highlight our friend's service. They listed the churches he had served and reminisced upon characteristic moments selected from rich relationships that spanned the decades.

We gave thanks to God and sang "For All the Saints" with a vigor appropriate to the hymn's words. Hearts heavy with grief, we greeted the pastor's widow and met his adult daughters, with their own children clinging to their skirts. Pastors mingled with pastors. Firm handshakes, spontaneous embraces, occasional laughter, the wiping of tears, and then each of us returned to our churches to continue our work.

Thirty minutes of reminiscence and thanksgiving cannot encompass a pastor's life. Our friend had served churches for more than thirty years. If only we could measure the despair lifted and guilt relieved, the hope restored and friendships sustained, the marriages revived and youths redeemed through his faithful work. The lives touched by him are incalculable—how many sickbed hands he held in prayer, how many human wills he pushed to new resolve, how many minds he enlivened with the imponderables of our faith, how many hearts he molded with love.

His weddings and funerals and baptisms fill church records, but no book could contain all the Sunday school classes, women's groups, prayer meetings, Bible studies, youth retreats, and board meetings shaped by his spirit and mind. Even such a list would not include the quiet conversations in hospital hallways, the intimate asides at picnics, the late night prayers over telephone lines, the tender embraces when no words were appropriate. Our brother left his fingerprints upon the souls of thousands.

But now death has come to him, as eventually to all of us.

What is the place of our striving in ministry? With less ambition, our friend's circle of influence might have been half as large. His energetic pursuit of service, his conscientious manner that led to late night sermon rewrites, his taste for excellence—these blessed his life, and through them, he served the Lord.

We wrestle with the mystery that the same energies of the soul that propel us to great service can send us spinning off the road. When we turn our ambitions back on ourselves and away from community, our circle of influence for the gospel shrinks to insignificance. Lonely for the families we have neglected and cut off from the community we have disregarded, we seek a happiness that eludes our grasping.

In each pastor is replicated, in small letters, the capital challenges of the centuries. The history of the church consists of successive excursions from the same starting point—the call, periods of doubt and times of hope, the need for community and the search to stand out, our desires for spiritual gifts and earthly goods, the shaping of our ambitions by both appetite and altruism. Each of us exercises skill and persistence to overcome, solve, and serve. Each of us seeks to create more than we consume, to give more than we have received. In the story of each of us is written the history of our faith.

God has poured into our lives the same motives of countless generations, aspiring through the ages to great service. We forge our ministry in the tension between our desire to serve others and our drive to serve ourselves.

We can so easily misdirect the energies of the soul that we call ambition. On our better days we know that our purpose is not acclaim, and it is not to outdo all the others. Our purpose is community; it is fidelity to our calling; it is evidence of lives changed—spirits comforted, hearts freed for love, minds open to the workings of grace.

If you or I were to die today, in seven years we would be remembered with fondness. Our families and friends would still feel the pain of our parting. In seventy years, we would be a dim memory in the minds of very few, a name over a short line on a genealogy chart.

Seven hundred years from now, there would be no trace of our names on any surviving civic or church record. No tombstone could be found to list us. Seven thousand years from now, there may be no record even of the 250-million-member society of which we are part. And yet seven thousand years is like a drop in the endless ocean of time.

When we contemplate such thoughts, a cold trickle of fear winds through our souls. We sense fully the weight of our earthly substance, our affinity with the dust from which we were formed. What is the place of our toil and striving?

Pastors die. Every pastor dies. After striving to their fullest, pushing, living, competing, pouring themselves into their work, they die. We touch thousands of lives, then the earth reclaims us all—our passions, our hopes, our fears, our failings. But one generation later, or at most two, no earthly memory remains of our work.

122

The fact is starkly simple: Our striving and achievements are unable to protect us from the ultimate reality that we do die and that all our works do follow us.

Perhaps it was while wrestling with the all-consuming power of death that these words were written: "All is vanity . . . what gain do they have from toiling for the wind?" (Eccl. 1:2*b*; 5:16). Or these: "As for mortals, their days are like grass; they flourish like a flower of the field; for the wind passes over it, and it is gone, and its place knows it no more" (Ps. 103:15-16).

In response, we can surrender to the bitter cynicism that life has no meaning, that all our ambitions are empty and all our work without purpose or consequence. Like ants mindlessly carrying their burdens, we fulfill our small roles until we die. Or we eat, drink, and are merry, not caring about the character of our striving.

Or we could fall into hopelessness, shrinking back in desperate and paralyzing fear, huddling over our capacities, terrified that we might use them up too soon. Fear turns us in upon ourselves.

Or we can cry out at the unfairness, the inherent injustice that turns life and work to sand and bone, that brings minds and achievements to dust.

That's the sting of death. If our significance derives from what we do, then what happens when we realize that our works do not have the power to outlive us, that they too are swallowed up in death?

But thanks be to God who gives us the victory! The significance of our lives cannot be fully expressed by what we do, what we achieve, or whether we are remembered. Certainly our value cannot be measured by how much higher some climb than others, or how much salary we earn.

Life finds its value from beyond our earthly lives, or not at all. We enjoy an imputed righteousness that is not earned or achieved. All of us are loved enough for Christ to die for us. Confrontation with our own mortality swings us full around to the necessity of grace. Meaning and purpose are not created by us, but received by us; not dependent upon our works, but accepted by our faith. The purpose of life comes from beyond ourselves. The value of our lives, whether we die young or old, infirm or productive, comes gift-like from God alone. Our ultimate significance grows out of the life, death, and resurrection of Jesus Christ.

Life is too short, our earthly frame too fragile, to spend our time crushing one another, competing and struggling toward the diminution of our abundance, in desperate search for the justification we can never create for ourselves, no matter how we try.

We find satisfaction in our work, joy and meaning, *but not salvation.* We dare not worship our work, but our work can become part of our worship of God.

—Robert Schnase
Ambition in Ministry

A SELF-EMPTIED HEART

Our vocation is to follow Christ on his downward path and become witnesses to God's compassion in the concreteness of our time and place. Our temptation is to let needs for success, visibility, and influence dominate our thoughts, words and actions to such an extent that we are trapped in the destructive spiral of upward mobility and thus lose our vocation. It is this lifelong tension between vocation and temptation that presents us with the necessity of formation. Precisely because the downward mobility of the way of the cross cannot depend on our spontaneous responses, we are faced with the question, "How do we reach conformity to the mind and heart of the self-emptying Christ?"

To follow Christ requires the willingness and determination to let his Spirit pervade all the corners of our minds and hearts and there make us into other Christs. Formation is transformation, and transformation means a growing conformity to the mind of Christ, who did not cling to his equality with God but emptied himself.

Thus discipleship cannot be realized without discipline. Discipline in the spiritual life, however, has nothing to do with the discipline of athletics, academic study, or job training, in which physical fitness is achieved, new knowledge is acquired, or a new skill is mastered. The discipline of the Christian disciple is not to master anything, but rather to be mastered by the Spirit. True Christian discipline is the human effort to create the space in which the Spirit of Christ can transform us into his image.

We may pay careful attention to the disciplines of the spiritual life, for without discipline, discipleship degenerates into a spiritualized form of upward mobility, which is far worse than straightforward secular ambition to make it to the top. . . .

The Discipline of the Heart

The discipline which leads us on the way of true discipleship and protects us against the temptations of upward mobility is the discipline of the heart. The discipline of the heart is the discipline of personal prayer. In the context of the liturgical life of the church, and supported by an ongoing meditation on the Word of God, personal prayer leads us not just to our own heart, but to the heart of God.

124

The discipline of the heart is probably the discipline we give up most easily. Entering into the solitude of our closet and standing there in the presence of our God, with nothing but our own nakedness, vulnerability, and sinfulness, requires an intense commitment to the spiritual life. Personal prayer is not rewarded by acclaim, does not translate into helpful projects, and only rarely leads to the inner experience of peace and joy. Yet, personal prayer is the true test of our vocation.

For us born activists, the discipline of the heart through which we strip ourselves of all scaffoldings and cry out in our misery to the God of mercy and compassion is a discipline of purification. If we indeed desire to see God, if we indeed want to see him in and through the humiliated Christ living among us, and if we indeed want to follow Christ wherever he leads us, we need a pure heart, a heart free from the "oughts" and "musts" of our world.

Jesus says, "When you pray, do not imitate the hypocrites: they love to say their prayers standing up in synagogues and at street corners for people to see them. I tell you solemnly, they have had their reward. But when you pray, go to your private room and when you have shut your door pray to your Father who is in that secret place, and your Father who sees all that is done in secret will reward you" (Matthew 6:1-4). To truly become men and women whose identities are hidden in God, we need to have the courage to enter empty-handed into the place of solitude.

There is nothing romantic about this. If we take the discipline of the heart seriously, we have to start by setting a time and a place aside when and where we can be with God and God alone, not once in a while, but regularly. We need to look at our agenda and reserve time for personal prayer so that we can say honestly and without hesitation to those who want to see us at that time, "I am sorry, but I have already made an appointment then and it cannot be changed."

For most of us it is very hard to spend a useless hour with God. It is hard precisely because by facing God alone we also face our own inner chaos. We come in direct confrontation with our restlessness, anxieties, resentments, unresolved tensions, hidden animosities, and long-standing frustrations. Our spontaneous reaction to all this is to run away and get busy again, so that we at least can make ourselves believe that things are not as bad as they seem in our solitude.

The truth is that things *are* bad, even worse than they seem. It is this painful stripping away of the old self, this falling away from all our old support systems that enables us to cry out for the unconditional mercy of God. When we do not run away in fear, but patiently stay with our struggles, the outer space of solitude gradually becomes an inner space, a space in our heart where we come to know the presence of the Spirit who has already been given to us. In the solitude of our heart we can listen to our question and—as the German poet Rilke says so beautifully—gradually grow, without even noticing it, into the answer.

The discipline of the heart is the discipline by which we create that inner space in which the Spirit of God can cry out in us "Abba, Father" (see Romans 8:15). Thus, through the discipline of the heart, we reach the heart of God. When we come to hear the heartbeat of God in the intimacy of our prayer, we realize that God's heart embraces all the sufferings of the world. We come to see that through Jesus Christ these burdens have become a light burden which we are invited to carry.

Prayer always leads us to the heart of God and the heart of the human struggle at the same time. It is in the heart of God that we come to understand the true nature of human suffering and come to know our mission to alleviate this suffering, not in our own name, but in the name of the one who suffered and through his suffering overcame all evil.

The discipline of the heart has its own special difficulties. There is the temptation to start hoping for personal revelations and personal sensations. There is the problem of not knowing if we hear God or just our own restlessness. There is the question of how to discern the direction in which the Spirit moves us. But before and above all these special difficulties, there is the simple difficulty of being faithful to the discipline itself. All this suggests that it might be a great help to have a personal spiritual director, especially when we are just starting to take our spiritual life seriously.

A spiritual director is a fellow Christian to whom we choose to be accountable for the discipline of our heart and from whom we may expect a firm commitment to pray for us. The simple fact that we have to reveal to another Christian with some regularity the status of our personal prayer life, and the simple knowledge that he or she is lifting us up to God with great love and care, can make all the difference in our spiritual development.

With someone on our side who keeps encouraging us to enter deeper through our own heart into the heart of God, we will also be much more free to be with others in their pains and to discover with them the presence of the healing God in our midst. Thus the discipline of the heart leads us on the path of compassion; that is, the downward path, which is the narrow road which leads to life (see Matthew 7:13). . . .

We are called to follow Christ on his downwardly mobile road, tempted to choose the broad path of success, notoriety, and influence, and challenged to subject ourselves to spiritual disciplines in order to gradually conform to the image of our Lord Jesus Christ.

Vocation, temptation, and formation are lifelong realities. We are called not once, but day in and day out, and we will never know for sure where we are being led. We are tempted at every moment of our day and night and we will never know precisely where our demons will appear. This lifelong tension between vocation and temptation opens up for us the difficult but promising task of listening to the church, the Book, and our spiritual director, thus discovering the real presence of God's Spirit within and among us.

We will never be without struggle. But when we persevere with hope, courage, and confidence, we will come to fully realize in our innermost being that through the downward road of Christ we will enter with him into his glory. So let us be grateful for our vocation, resist our temptations, and be ever committed to a life of ongoing formation.

—Henri Nouwen
Sojourners

— THE LAST TEMPTATION OF THE CHURCH —

Life is a tenacious thing. I remember when first I learned that, I was a boy, maybe ten years old, chopping cotton. I don't know if that means a lot to some of you. You have to hoe, and it's hot, and you're in a field cutting weeds out of the cotton. I came upon a snake. I didn't take time to figure out what kind of snake it was, because a snake comes in several categories, all of which are called snake. I killed the snake—or at least I thought I killed the snake, but I had not. Chop, chop, chop. Finally I went to my father and I said, "I killed a snake, but it won't die." And he said, "You'll have to take the snake and hang it on the fence, and it will die at sundown." I didn't know snakes didn't die 'til sundown. I took the snake and hanged it on a fence, and the rest of the day I looked toward the fence and the tail of the snake continued to move, haunting me with life.

And when Jesus said, "I'm going, I will be killed," no wonder Simon Peter screamed in his face and said "No! We can survive." And in that bitter exchange, not bitter so much as loud and violent exchange, finally Jesus said, "Hush, no more of this. You represent to me a tempter. Get behind me. The voice that insists upon survival! survival! survival! No! In fact you're wrong about me, Simon Peter, in fact, you're wrong about yourself, because the church that follows me must also take up the cross." "Oh, no. You mean the church might die?" "Yes." With one hand he took his own cross, with the other he handed a cross to the church, and the church has said with Simon Peter ever since: "No, no, we can survive! We know ways to survive. We can survive. I know attendance is dropping, I know the budget's going down. I know the public press is making fun of the church. I know they talk about mainstream Christianity being on the way out. I know that, but we can survive."

127

You can write to Colorado Springs and get these survival kits. And there are some tapes by motivators, and there's the possibility thinking and all that. We can make it. We can cut back on the budget a little bit. We may have to take some of the money out of outreach and put it in a savings account, in case we get a little low. I know we'll have to cut back on staff, we'll have to reduce our program. But we can survive. We can survive. We can do like some of the churches and have special events. I notice a big booming church in Florida. Every once in a while they'll have a beauty queen come in and say a little word for Jesus. "A Miss Ochra from South Texas will now say a little witness for us." They have basketball players, seven foot eight, come and say a word of witness, and the crowds are great. And there was a church in Atlanta—they tell me the place was full—that had a midget who was a professional yo-yoer who did all these marvelous things with a yo-yo and quoted scripture for an hour all during the act. And they say the place was packed. Now listen, we can survive! There are ways to survive!

I know, I know as well as you do, that there is a lot of death around the church, a lot of deadliness about the church. You experience it, I experience it. I recall reading about Charles Dickens once attending a gathering of clerics. And he said the meeting was so dead, so boring, so dull, that after a couple of hours he said, "May I make a suggestion? Let's move over to a table and join hands and sit in silence and see if we can commune with the living." We all know that feeling.

But I am not here to read the coroner's report about the church, to hang crepe on the door of half-filled sanctuaries. I have not myself heard the flap of the condor's wing over the church. In fact, the whole idea of the church taking a cross and possibly dying, is not a welcome one for me. I have a tendency to think of the church as immortal! immortal! immortal! It is hard to say, "The church is dead." Just as it was hard for them to say, "Jesus is dead." The church has never been able to pronounce that "Jesus is dead!" Even on that awful Saturday, the church could not say, "Jesus is dead." They thought up stories: "You know the one they really crucified was the one carrying the cross, Simon of Cyrene, that's the one that was crucified." "Do you know that sponge they passed to him on the cross? It was a plan. It had a drug in it. He would pass out. His bodily functions would recede almost to imperceptible depth, and they would take him down and revive him. He didn't die! He didn't die! No, Jesus! Survival is the word." I feel the same way about the church. But I know this. There is something faulty in the thinking that says the death of Jesus is the life of the world, and the death of the church is the end of the world. No.

When you move to lead the churches across this land and around the world, pressure will be put on you as though the number one item on the agenda is survival at any cost. Survival! survival! survival! And I hope in that pressure for success and booming anything—let's get them here again!—I do hope you will hear his voice. "Get behind me, tempter. Take up your cross. You must give your life." What does that mean, give your life? I don't know. I think it means to be willing to empty your pockets for somebody else's children. I think it means to treat as mother and father those who are not really your mother and father. I think it means to claim as brother and sister people to whom you are not kin. I think it means to reach out and touch untouchable people as far as our society is concerned. I think it means to sit at table with people who live far outside the tight social circle of some of your friends. Break bread together. It means to be a voice for moral values in a culture that will immediately accuse you of sinking into a bunch of moralistic thinking. It means to witness for Jesus Christ when evangelism is being laughed at everywhere. It means being an advocate, being an advocate to speak the gospel as though something were at stake. Not stand up and just describe how it is on one hand and how it is on the other, as though we were serving afternoon tea to the pros and cons of every issue. To advocate! It means to continue to give money to others even when the paint is peeling in the sanctuary. I think it means that. And if you go that way, there will be leaders in your own church who will say, "Look, this is suicide. We're losing. This is suicide." And you'll have to decide whether it is suicide, or giving your life. Who can say?

—Fred B. Craddock
The Princeton Seminary Bulletin

— RADICAL OPTIMISM —

When Jesus as teacher, as disciple-maker, desires that everyone should be like himself—and this is the goal of every sincere teacher—it means that he wants us to experience his freedom, his interior freedom from all of these inhibitions and fears and cravings and clutchings we've been talking about. He wants us to enjoy his self-realization, his union with the Source of Being, whom he calls Father. It's his own interior experience that he wants to share.

This means that the rest of us are to have this kind of experience. Whatever is reported of Jesus, therefore, is to be replicated in us. Just go through the Gospels and find out what he is like. It's a revelation of what is in store for you, what is expected of you, what is promised to you, and what you in your profoundest reality always already are. What he experiences in his consciousness, we are to experience in ours. We are to enter

129

into his very heart, the center of his being. Surely this must be what his thorough self-gift means, what being "with him where he is" means, what hearing everything that he has heard from the Father means, what being engrafted into his life so that his blood flows in our veins means.

Entering into the heart of Jesus means also entering into our own heart, the center of our being, the core of our existence. Can we find this in experience, actually do it? Yes, but everything superficial must be laid aside.

We are coming now to the mystical detachment. We are not talking about the usual abstinences, about the avoidance of unkindness to a neighbor, and so forth. We are now going to get into it much more deeply. There are layers and layers of superficiality. Everything, before you come to the heart itself, is comparatively superficial.

Let us retrace briefly the steps we have taken to arrive here. Saved by our acceptance of God's unconditional love for us, we are freed from the need to insist on our personal pleasure and power. We do not make the attainment of possessions and privileges the chief goal of our life. We do not concentrate on the pursuit of bodily pleasures, stimulations, and comforts. We do not identify with our success or failure in our career. We do not refuse to rejoice in God's life because of disappointments in human relations.

Many of the descriptions of the superficial self have thus been stripped off. But they may have been replaced with some new ones: I belong to such a culture, such a religious tradition; I have such a role or office in my tradition; I follow such a spiritual path. An even if these have been transcended, we are left with our sense of our own personality and with our ideas of how the God-world relation is structured: our psychology and our theology. These are much harder to "unknow," and many people hold that we are not to give up identifying with them at all.

Probably not very many Christians would be willing to do what is reported of a certain Zen adept. He was well known as a master in their tradition. But he had in the vestibule of his home a calligraphy hanging on the wall, a beautiful piece of writing, which read: "I have long since forgotten what is Zen Buddhism." He had followed beyond the pointing finger and had seen the moon.

But what else is the contemplative life for? It is where the great risks can be faced, where folkloric religion can be outgrown and the naked Reality entered into by the naked spirit. In the depths of the contemplative life, there should no longer be any secrets, any euphemisms, any tales told to children, but the way should be clear to find the Real beyond finite descriptions.

—Beatrice Bruteau
Radical Optimism

Do I Have a Future in the Church?
— I WILL PLACE A NEW SPIRIT WITHIN YOU —

I shall give you a new heart and put a new spirit within you. I shall remove the heart of stone from your bodies and give you a heart of flesh. (Ezekiel 36:26)

If there is one phenomenon that characterizes contemporary religious search, it is the quest for an authentic spirituality. Feminist, monastic, ecumenical, creation-centered, spirituality of struggle: Each has its proponents and advocates. Each has its literature and its pursuits. Charges of pantheism, escapism, activism, elitism shadow some of these quests. Whether the focus is a renewed discipleship, a healing of dualisms, or a search for personal meaning, the issue is "spirituality."

It is unfortunate that this abstraction, spirituality, has become the common parlance. The potential for misinterpretation is obvious. For some it signals a split between the physical or the natural and that which is spiritual. For others it connotes an interior movement away from life's realities and human tragedies. For still others it is a private journey of prayer and conversion. Its ambiguity has led today's disciples to turn it into "holistic spirituality."

The Scriptures are more concrete and perhaps more accurate. "I will place a new spirit within you" (Ezekiel 36:26). "Renew a right spirit within me" (Psalm 51). "My spirit rejoices in God my Savior" (Luke 1:47). "Into your hands I commend my spirit" (Luke 23:46). "If you do not have the spirit of Christ, you do not belong to Christ" (Romans 8:9).

There is nothing abstract or vague about Ezekiel's "stony hearts." We all know the reality: hardheartedness, indifference, an incapacity to feel, to respond, to love. I am inhabited, says Jesus in Luke 4:18, by a spirit, pervaded by it, so that the entirety of my life is evidence of this occupying spirit. To be possessed by a spirit is to be consumed, taken over. The spirit of our lives is our total self, who we really are. It is the self that is not confined to time and place. It is the self that spans all our experiences and responses. It is the self that is our truest being. Spirituality is the process that leads to true selfhood. If we are Christians, it is a movement into Christ's path.

—Joan Puls
Seek Treasures in Small Fields

— HERE AM I, LORD, USE ME! —

"Blessed are the meek, for they will inherit the earth." Of all the Beatitudes, this is the hardest to take, the most difficult to swallow. The difficulty here, of course, is with the word *meek.* I mean, who wants to be meek today? It sounds so weak and wimpy, so syrupy.

I once heard about a little boy who became frustrated with his mother one day because she kept referring to him as her "little lamb."

Finally the four-year-old couldn't take it anymore and he said, "Mama, I don't want to be your little lamb. I want to be your little *tiger!"*

That's the way it is with most of us. We would be ashamed of being called "meek" in the way we understand the word today. Meek people and meek nations are those with no guts, no strength, no backbone. Some "blessedness" may await them in heaven, we think, but here on earth they are pushed around and kicked in the teeth. Today, meekness is a synonym for weakness.

But when Jesus spoke this third Beatitude, that's not what he had in mind at all. For Jesus, *meekness* meant "obedience to God." Throughout the Bible, the word *meek* is used to describe those people who have committed themselves totally to doing the will of God and to being God's servants—those who have yielded themselves completely to God—like putty in God's hands.

It's helpful to remember that in the Old Testament, Moses (of all people) was called "the meekest" of men. Now, think about that. It was Moses to whom God appeared in the burning bush. It was Moses whom God called upon to lead Israel out of slavery. It was Moses who courageously laid his life on the line by standing before Pharaoh and saying, "Let my people go!" It was Moses who received the Ten Commandments. It was Moses who brought the people out of Egypt through the Red Sea. It was Moses who led the people through the wilderness, through battle, and through discouragement, toward the Promised Land.

No question about it—Moses was one of the strongest leaders and most courageous characters in the whole Bible. Yet when we come to the twelfth chapter of the book of Numbers in the King James Version of the Bible, we find these revealing words: "Now the man Moses was very meek, above all the men which were upon the face of the earth." Moses was a man of meekness because he realized how much he needed God, and he gave himself completely to God. He obeyed God. He trusted God. He served God. He did God's will—and that's what it means to be meek. It's the opposite of arrogance, haughtiness, pride, and selfishness. The meek are those who humbly yield themselves to God, to be used as God's tools any way and anywhere God should choose. There is great strength in that.

—James W. Moore
When All Else Fails . . . Read the Instructions

— GROWING IN GRACE —

The biblical promise that if we truly seek, we shall find God, is the basis for the journey of the spiritual life. In spite of the difficulties along the way, the times of dryness when nothing seems to be happening, the discouragement and distraction that come to us all, and the times of falling back and wondering if we have made any progress at all, the journey is one from which we cannot turn back. The testimony of the saints of all the ages is that the journey is worth it; that God really is love; and that the love God offers is the most important reality that can be known by any of us. Such knowledge enables a person to have tremendous power to take what happens, to surmount great difficulties, and to grow in the face of tragedy and deep disappointment.

The fruit of the spiritual life is not easily attained. The process of growing in grace is sometimes difficult. It requires persistence which never comes easily for any of us. The old part of us, the part that wants to go it alone and maintain control, keeps asserting itself. There are times when we want to go back to being unaware and half dead. God requires honesty from us, and such honesty can be painful. Because God knows us better than we know ourselves, pretending will not work. God's knowledge of us demands that we come to terms with who we really are.

In a beautiful summary of the process of growth in grace, Flora Wuellner says this: "As we are healed and pulled together into wholeness, we are shown many things that we had not seen before. We are shown feelings we have had, but which have been repressed. We are shown things we have done, judgments we have made during our days of blindness and insensitivity. We are shown relationships in a new light, and facts to which we had not awakened. And as we wake and see, decisions about what we see begin to rise in freshness and power."

The goal of the Christian life is union with Christ, but such union is only dimly and occasionally realized in this life by most of us. Nevertheless, the pilgrimage toward the goal is one of joyful discovery that Christ is with us whether or not we realize that presence. We are given new opportunities for relationship with others along the way. We find new possibilities within us that we had not thought possible. The adventure of the Christian life is one that demands all we can give it. But the testimony of the ages is that the goal of the adventure is well worth the struggle. The hungry heart of the pilgrim is fed along the way.

—Howard L. Rice
Reformed Spirituality

— SIMPLICITY —

The last task that I have experienced as central to our growing in Christ is the one that is probably the most difficult. How, in a world as complex as our own, can we achieve a level of simplicity that reveals the Christ in us? The answer, of course, is that we don't achieve it. It is a gift that comes as the fruit of a long and intimate relationship with the Lord. We all know people whose lives reflect this quality. Simplicity reflects an inner wisdom and a comfortableness with the wholeness of life that is bred in solitude and expressed through a certain spontaneity and joyousness that enriches every gathering in which it is found. It affects the way we live, what we need, and the way we relate to the world around us.

Although simplicity is not a quality of life that we can turn on or turn off at will, it is nevertheless a spiritual concern we can respond to. I met a person the other day who, after a few minutes' conversation, made me feel that I had known her all my life. She had a capacity to be present to me with such transparency that I felt immediately connected. As I reflect on the experience, I realize that I saw in this person a simplicity that had come from clearing away the things that often prevent people from connecting with one another—restlessness, self-absorption, hidden agendas, and the like. For those brief moments I experienced this woman for what she was, and my life was enriched. She had no need to impress me or to influence me, hence she was able to be present without deception or guile. We develop this quality first of all by wanting it, by practicing it, and by opening ourselves to what God can do when we get out of the way.

Addressing the task of more authentically reflecting the simplicity of the Gospel, therefore, means addressing how we pray and how we live and how we relate to others. Our aim is not intensity but the joyous freedom that is found in Christ. "Take my yoke upon you, and learn from me," Jesus says, "for I am gentle and lowly in heart, and you will find rest for your souls. For my yoke is easy, and my burden is light" (Matthew 11:29-30; RSV). Herein lies the paradox of simplicity.

—James C. Fenhagen
Ministry and Solitude

— DIVINE THERAPY —

The myths of modernism are dying all around us. Our sophistication and complexity are self-destructing. For several hundred years we were convinced in the West that progress, human reason, and higher technology would resolve the human dilemma. They clearly have not. Without denying the gifts of mind and science, we now doubt their messianic promise. More analysis is not necessarily more wisdom, and more options are not necessarily freedom. The accumulation of things is not likely to bring more happiness, and time saved is rarely used for contemplation.

Progress has too often been at the expense of the earth, and human reason has too easily legitimated war, greed, and the pursuit of a private agenda, while technology pays those who serve it, especially the moguls of militarism and medicine. Our philosophy of progress has led us to trust in our own limitlessness and in our future more than in the quality and the mystery of the *now*. Religion at its best is always concerned about the depth and breadth and wonder of things. In this sense we have become an impatient and irreligious people. The paschal mystery, the yin and yang of all reality, is outshouted by the quite recent and unproven slogan: "we can have it all!". . .

The cost, of course, is the problem. The almost impossible task of the Church is to offer both the promise and the price—simultaneously. Promise without price becomes sweet sentimentality; price without promise becomes shame, burden, and grief. We have enough of both. But who will point us back to the "condition of complete simplicity"? And who wants to go? I do believe there is a divine therapy both for the individual and for the Church. It is the radical contemplative stance. Aldous Huxley rightly called it "the perennial philosophy." It is the return to simplicity that comes from lots of good looking and good listening. I will go so far as to say, "There is no other way." But the cost is not less than everything:

> To come to the pleasure you have not
> you must go by a way in which you enjoy not.
> To come to the knowledge you have not
> you must go by a way in which you know not.
> To come to the possesion you have not
> you must go by a way in which you possess not.
> To come to be what you are not
> you must go by a way in which you are not.
> (St. John of the Cross, *The Ascent of Mt. Carmel*)

—Richard Rohr
Simplicity

— NO HITCHHIKING ON ANOTHER'S SPIRITUAL JOURNEY —

In Peter Ustinov's drama *Beethoven's Tenth*, a resurrected Beethoven evaluates a young composer, Pascal Fauldgate. Beethoven tells the musician that there is nothing wrong with his technique. The problem is that "you have nothing to say, and you say it quite well." Likewise, it doesn't matter how eloquent the sermon is if the preacher has nothing to share. Ministry is not just a matter of gifts and graces; it also has to do with faith and the fruits of faith. The questions John Wesley asked his preachers in 1746 still need to be raised:

> Have they gifts, as well as grace, for the work? Have they a clear, sound understanding; a right judgment in the things of God; a just conception of salvation by faith? Do they speak justly, readily, clearly?

> Have they fruit? Have any been truly convinced of sin and converted to God, and are believers edified by their preaching?

The political mystic understands that one cannot live on borrowed faith alone. No one can hitchhike on another's spiritual journey. We can have companions along the way, but ultimately each minister must live and die by his or her own faith experience. The intimate association with the Divine is a self-transcending, all encompassing moment of mystery never quite analyzable or communicatable. Touched by God's grace, we are never quite the same, even when the absence of God seems stronger than the divine presence.

The contemplation of God is good in and of itself. One need not commend a life of devotion for utilitarian reasons. Contemplative prayer, however, is practical; it is divine therapy for the human condition. The testimony of the mystics is that the contemplative vision of God leads to "metanoia," a conversion of the heart. Such a conversion, argues William Johnston, must expand the social vision. Johnston calls for conversions to poverty, to peace, and to justice, giving up self-made security, living the way of compassion, and trusting in God.

The immediacy of the mystic's experience of God has a sustaining power among the struggles and defeats of pastoral and prophetic action. It is no wonder that the great social and political activists of the Christian faith have always been women and men who have cultivated the spiritual arts. Prayer and politics were inseparable. Often these political mystics have known the intimacy of suffering. Having wrestled, like Jacob, they emerge with a limp and speak the language of Job.

> I know that thou canst do all
>   things,
>   and that no purpose of thine can
>   be thwarted.
> "Who is this that hides counsel
>   without knowledge?"

Do I Have a Future in the Church?

> Therefore I have uttered what I did
> not understand,
> things too wonderful for me, which
> I did not know.
>
> (Job 42:2-3)

Martin E. Marty has observed that "the religious person and community cannot dip into the endowment and live off the interest and the principal of a spiritual capital in which they did not invest." One, can, however, benefit significantly from devotional disciplines and reading the great mystics. Becoming soul friends with the spiritual masters can provide needed illumination along ministry's way. My own mentor, Walter G. Muelder, wrote in his Boston University *festschrift* that mystics of the East and West

> have helped me in self-examination, in sorting out motives, in ecumenical understanding, in handling personal attacks, in radical dissent from established institutions, in awareness of the spiritual continuity in the Christian tradition, in distinguishing genuine from superficial piety, and in developing the trust which lies at the heart of faith . . . for the life of devotion is both serenity and struggle.

Bridging the gap between the human and the divine, the finite and the infinite, the now and the "wholly other" is an uncertain and unending quest. The moments most of us feel close to God are relatively few, and the times we would claim to have had religious experiences are relatively far between. The most famous political mystics of the church have acknowledged that they, too, have known what Saint John the Divine called "the dark night of the soul" and what contemporary psychologists might call "burnout." The struggle for spiritual wholeness has always been a time of wrestling with the limitation of one's own inner self and what we understand to be the perfection and expectation of God.

God, for the political mystic, is not to be found only in private or community prayer, but by plunging into the agonies and anguish, the quagmires and quicksands of life. In Sean O'Casey's autobiography, *Rose and Crown*, there is a delightful Irish argument about God. When the question is pushed whether God is a Catholic or a Protestant, the answer is neither. O'Casey responds, God

> may be but a *shout in the street*. . . . When God is a shout in the street, the shout is never a creed. . . . It might be a shout of people for bread, as in the French Revolution; or for the world's ownership, as in the Russian Revolution; or it might just be a drunken man in the night on a deserted street, shouting out Verdi's *O'Leonora*, unsteadily meandering his way homewards.

In the past, too much talk about spirituality has stressed life-denial rather than life-affirmation. "Repression, not expression; guilt, not pleasure; heaven, not this life; sentimentality, not justice; mortification, not developing of talents," says Matthew Fox, have been "the earmarks of Western spirituality." Prayer has been understood more in terms of withdrawal from life than engagement with life. Often, in search of the spiritual, we have turned private and inward or locked ourselves within the church walls, only to discover that others have found God in the vitality and voices of the street.

Dorothy Day is said to have seen Christ in everyone. She found Christ in bowery derelicts, in Nazis, in Communists, and in cardinals who admired Senator Joseph McCarthy. She loved everyone who detested everyone else. She refused to fit anyone's philosophy or political mold and thereby discovered spirituality in the secular and the divine in the mundane. Yes, for the political mystic God is a shout in the streets—the shouts of joy and sorrow, the shouts of hope and of pain, the shouts of our neighbor and of the stranger, the shouts of the mighty and the meek—the shouts of the loud and "the least of these my brethren."

—Donald E. Messer
Contemporary Images of Christian Spirituality

— THE UNSPOKEN CONTRACT —

The reality is that the vast majority of persons in a typical congregation do not want themselves or their world to be transformed by the gospel. Instead, they want the minister to help them make life easier to manage while they and their world stay the same in every important respect. The gospel says that we and the world orders in which we live must be changed to enjoy its blessings. . . .

Typically, church members, clergy and lay, are most deeply committed to family, career, and standard of living. Whenever we are challenged by competing values, these three prevail.

Caught in the backwash of broken dreams of being change agents, young clergy shift toward pursuit of career as an alternative future. Advocacy of personal and social transformation fades as a major preoccupation of ministry. Career becomes the dominant eschatology for the profession. An unspoken contract gets struck. If we exert ourselves to provide what the institutional church wants at local and denominational levels, we will be rewarded with career advancement. From this point on, our ministries tend to be driven by pursuit of career rather than by passion for change.

To retain or recover our original dream in the face of career eschatology we will need to take certain steps. Discipleship nurture for clergy will mean clustering with other clergy who are resisting this takeover of the eschatology of career. This disciple circle will need to find together the means of grace to purge its members of domination by the big three until some more faithful form of ministry emerges. I am confident that can happen—but not unless clergy arrange for themselves a nurturing process. . . .

I hope I have not drawn too dark a picture of the first and formative years as a pastoral leader. For many readers what I have described will not fit their experience. All my reading and observation tells me that it is an accurate picture of what happens to most of us. It is nothing any of us ought to feel ashamed of. The culture and the institution to which we belong prescribe it for us. It is merely the churchly version of what happens to most adult males in our culture. I doubt there is much we can do about it until it happens to us, given our lack of warning and preparation. What matters is that we take vigorous action when we come to realize what is happening.

If this description of the predicament of the minister does not strike a chord of recognition now, eventually it will. Perhaps we may be fifteen to twenty years into ministry. That is how long it usually takes for career advancement to reach its peak. That point in our careers is like the experience of the first disciples when their career dreams vanished at the arrest of Jesus and the prospect of his execution. They had done what Jesus asked in the hope of a career in the coming kingdom. From their point of view it seemed that Jesus had defaulted on their deal. They forsook him and fled.

We experience a similar sense of betrayal. We have contracted with the institutional church for career advancement. Then the institution fails to keep its part of the bargain. Sometime in our forties or fifties we realize that we will rise no higher. There will be no larger or more challenging parishes to lead. How we respond to this jolt to our hopes will determine our path of maturing from then on. If we respond appropriately, *this time in our careers may usher in a golden era* of usefulness and satisfaction.

—Neill Q. Hamilton
Maturing in the Christian Life

— SOUL FRIEND —

We are men and women with scattered and fragmented hearts. I have left parts of myself behind with family and friends in places which I scarcely remember. The friend of my soul is the one who guards and honors these bits and pieces which I call "me." I have also sent fragments ahead of myself and God knows where they are. My friend knows of them and walks with me towards them. My heart is on its way home and I have placed it in the keeping of others, for it is only with them that I can find my way home. This companionship is the setting of my social and political life as well as my private and personal one. The belief that we are all fellow pilgrims and companions has far-reaching social and political implications. Friendship has a public side, especially Christian friendship which is for the healing of the world. God is friendship and this means that we are called to be friends in him. Not that we can be close friends with millions of people across the earth. We can, however, share in the friendliness of God and thereby build up the network of interconnections which bind God's friends together.

And what is it all for? Again we find a clue in *Godric:*

> Oh thou who art the sparrow's friend . . . have mercy on this world that knows not even when it sins. O holy dove, descend and roost on Godric here so that a heart may hatch in him at last. Amen.

Companionship is for the hatching of our hearts. It is for the bringing home of our scattered and fragmented selves, for the making of a heart at home with itself. When I am truly at home with myself in God, I can then be truly present to my friends and fellow pilgrims.

It is all very simple. Companionship is your hand stretched out to me when I am frozen and lost. It is the film of sweat between pressed cheeks. It is your seeing in me *the terrific thing.* It is my waiting attentively on your hurt and listening to your fears. It is the tears, the laughter and the joy we share *in the Lord.* It is walking together the way of the cross and living together in the power of the resurrection. In short God's life is our life.

—Alan Jones
Exploring Spiritual Direction

— REFORM AND RENEWAL —

The church is the family of God, a visible, historical, human community called to nurture its people in the Gospel tradition so that they might live under the judgment and inspiration of that tradition to the end that God's will is done and God's community comes. The church is the body of Christ, a hidden, prophetic creature of God's spirit, an instrument of God's transforming power, and a witness to God's continuing revelation in history.

It is one church, a paradox to the mind: sinful, yet holy; divided, yet one; continuously in need of reform, yet the bearer of God's transforming eternal Word; a human institution and a holy community; a disparate assembly of baptized sinners living, sometimes unconsciously, by grace, but also an intentional, obedient, steadfast, faithful company of converted, visible saints; a mystery even to its members, who are aware, nevertheless, in often incomprehensible ways, that the church has a mission in the world and a ministry to those who by birth or decision find themselves, not entirely by choice, within that family which bears the name Christian.

Today you and I find ourselves living within some poor expressions of this one, holy, catholic, and apostolic church. It can be confusing and trying. There are moments when the church seems to be among the most bankrupt, hopeless, of institutions. And yet there are other times when we are aware that the meaning and purpose of life is dependent upon this fragile community of faith and doubt, of faithfulness and faithlessness. The history of the church seems to be a story of great truths revealed and lost, heights of faith realized and forgotten, prophetic actions demonstrated and denied.

Today as in days past our common life and witness in the church is mixed. Yet there are signs of hope. Among Christian churches—Protestant, Roman, Orthodox—there is a worldwide movement toward mutual recognition and collaboration. Christians and Jews have made a first step toward reconciliation. Attitudes toward the world's other faith communities are more positive and respectful. Reform in the liturgy is reuniting separated sisters and brothers and transforming congregations. Popular piety and civil religion no longer are accepted uncritically. Christians and the churches are increasingly alert to the pressing social problems of the day. New understandings have emerged from these critical judgments the church has brought against itself. Here and there, new spirit has erupted among the faithful and the ministry of the laity has come into its own.

But that is not the whole picture. There are signs of despair. Tensions between the generations, the sexes, the races continue. Tremendous upheavals in the world and the emergence of new moral dilemmas leave many troubled and adrift. Change within and without the church has caused disorientation, confusion, and estrangement. New splits have occurred. Spirituality—the experience of life with God—has for many reached a new low. Growing economic trials and tribulations and a lack of spiritual leadership confound the church. Anti-intellectualism increases. Fewer persons attend the rituals of the church. Among many persons throughout the world the church has lost its credibility. Decisions on political, social, and economic life divide the church. And a new pietism has surfaced to insulate the church from the world.

People are confused. They lack a sense of corporate identity. They are without an agreed-upon authority to which they can appeal and debate their differences. For some, the church is best understood in terms of doctrine in which the Scriptures and tradition are normative. Their primary concern is that all Christians assent to right belief. For others, the church is best understood in terms of religious experience in which the presence of the Holy Spirit and its gifts are normative. Their primary concern is that all Christians unite in prayer, fellowship, and an openness to the Spirit. For still others, the church is best understood as a social institution, either supporting personal needs or engaging in corporate service and action on behalf of humane causes in the society. Their primary concern is that the church serve human needs. The integration of these three understandings might appear easy in theory, but proves in practice to be extremely difficult.

Secular journalists, observing the confused self-image of the church and its mixed manifestations ask, as did the editors of *Newsweek*: "Has the Church Lost Her Soul?" It is an interesting question. But the answer, of course, is an unequivocal no! The soul of the church is not to be found in doctrine, in religious experience, or in outward forms or manifestations. The soul of the church is Jesus Christ. We cannot domesticate this Jesus in the church by our dogmatic affirmations, by our ecclesiastical systems, or by our lives of subjective individualism. We cannot base Christian faith on a wave of religious emotion, philosophical doctrine, or organizational development. Nor will we be helped by those who wish to embrace uncritically modern psychology or some other social science. A false modernity is no answer.

We can't ignore the obvious: There simply is no Christianity without Christ. To be Christian the church must affirm Jesus Christ as Lord. Christianity does not exist merely wherever humanity is realized. Humanity is realized outside Christianity. A Christian church is not any group of persons who strive to live a decent life in order to gain salvation. That too can be found outside the church. A Christian is not just any person of faith and good will. Only someone for whom the life, death, and resurrection of Jesus Christ is ultimately decisive may be called a Christian. Only a human community of which the same can be said may be called a church. Christianity only exists where the memory of this Christ is alive and his presence made real day by day in the being—the thought, feeling, and action—of persons and their community of faith.

But it isn't enough that we sing or say that Jesus Christ is Lord. We need to be clear about which Jesus we have made decisive in our lives, which Jesus we have made the authority for our faith. For the Christian, it is the Jesus of history; the Jesus with a simple and clear message: There is one God who acts in history and has an intention for creation, namely a world of peace, justice, unity, equity, and the health and well being of all. Jesus further proclaimed the coming of God's community. He announced that God's cause will, in spite of contrary evidence, prevail; that the future belongs to God. This same Jesus proclaimed one supreme norm for all human life: God's will, which was not a law or laws, but a way of being faithful. God's will, when it is done, will realize God's intentions for creation. Jesus, therefore, was biased toward those who were denied God's intentions, but he identified himself with all people and their needs. He acted on behalf of the sick, weak, lame, hurt, and oppressed. But he also sought out the heretics, the hypocrites, and the immoral, bringing them both judgment and mercy and thereby converting them to newness of life.

All this was good news and an example of life lived in unity with God and God's will. Still he was killed. But God did not permit his death to end his life. So it was that the little community who followed him and called him Rabbi experienced amidst their doubt that the crucified is living, that his death was dying into God. Jesus, the one seemingly forsaken by God, lives with, through, and in God. Thus is the cross an event of salvation and the resurrection a witness to God's transforming power. Only then was the church formed. Jesus is the Christ, God's Word (action) in history. And the church is the community of persons who profess in word and deed their faith in Jesus Christ. We Christians bear his name, are set apart through baptism in his name, sustained by his spirit so as to keep alive his memory and vision, and united at his family meal so as to know his presence and to be empowered by his grace. Christ is the soul of the church.

What does this mean for the church? It means that the church must ever be Catholic in substance and Protestant in spirit. In Jesus Christ the universal, eternal authority for Christian faith and life is given and the tradition shaped. Continuity with the Word of God in Jesus Christ must be protected and maintained. Still, because this divine Word is held in human vessels, a prophetic judgment upon and continual reform of our words and deeds are essential to the church's life. We who affirm our faith in Jesus Christ owe a radical obedience to God's coming community and are accountable to God's will. So it is that we must always be reforming and renewing our faith and commitment, our words and deeds, our common life and mission.

A renewed concentration on Jesus Christ will provide us with a common ground for judging and inspiring our lives. Together we can reform our limited and particular understandings and ways. We need to defend the responsibility of preserving and communicating the faith while not

143

neglecting our responsibility continually to examine it afresh and correct our ways in the light of our new understandings. Thereby will we be faithful. Church renewal and reform are essential to faithful life. A church that is faithful to Jesus Christ will be closer to God and at the same time closer to humanity; in uniting religious experience with prophetic action the church becomes more Christian.

—John H. Westerhoff III
Inner Growth, Outer Change

— HOPE FOR THE CHURCH —

The church is an exercise in inner fitness, in finding the place where the seams come together. Life in the church is exactly what the scripture says: It is treasure encased in earthen vessels. Life in the church is a treasure hunt for the integrity of the inner and the outer. In these latter days of church decline and church fear yelling above church grace, our inner, hungry hope is much larger than our outer experience.

We too often go to church hungry and leave hungry. If I were to describe our current stage of spiritual fitness, I think I would use the word *cleft*. Cleft, as in "rock of ages, cleft for me. Let me hide myself in thee." We have fallen out of grace. We are desperate for a place to hide and to rest and to hold on to whatever integrity we can patch together. But God keeps pushing us out of our cleft into the church, the world, the unclefted places. And so we fall in and out of grace—and are caught at each new level of difficulty by a new cleftedness! The interstices are both trouble and promise, like the woman who greets you the next morning and says, "You know I had the same awful experience you had at that meeting last night. What shall we do about it?" She becomes our church, the place where we can rest before the next battle. Without her, we would never return to the next meeting. Because of her, we can't not go.

I am beginning to realize that the more I fall, the more I am caught, that God puts clefts in the rocks. Whether we are climbing up, or falling down, the image works. There are places in the Rock of Ages where we can get what we want, but there aren't that many. . . .

I probably stay with the church because there are fewer and fewer places to take my longing for a good wrestling match with the poetry of our inner battles. I had thought church would be such a place, where we would be so hungry for justice and juice, music and dancing, that there would be no doubt about the depth of our fights. We would always know they would be about God and what God wanted through us in the world.

144

More of my battles are about whether we should serve cookies or sandwiches at the coffee hour. Or what to do with rambunctious children. Or who keeps the church kitchen cleaner, the "outsiders" or the "insiders." They have a very external, rather than internal, feel. And yet, who am I to tell God how to test me? These may be the battles of my longing. And it may be more up to me than I even realize to elevate and deepen these battles, so that the treasure hunt for God is of a piece with them. I know that I will be clefted along the way.

—Donna Schaper
Hard Times

Blessed are those who in serving thy church
   remember that they are serving thee.
Blessed are those who in doing charity
   remember that they are giving to thee.
Blessed are those who as they savor the good
   fruits of the earth
   remember from whose hand they received them. *Amen.*
     —Edward Tyler
      Prayers in Celebration of the Turning Year

RETREAT  PATTERN

Prayer for Guidance

O Divine Love, who calls and sends all who follow you, help me in this time apart to once more hear your voice. Grant grace to hear your voice calling and sending me, and grant faith enough to respond in obedience. *Amen.*

Silent Listening

Scripture Reading

Isaiah 6:1-9*a*; 1 Samuel 3:1-18; Luke 9:1-6; Luke 10:1-12; Acts 9:10-19

What does each passage tell me about God?
What does each passage tell me about myself?
What does each passage tell me about my ministry?

Spiritual Reading

Reflection

Mealtime, Rest, Recreation

Journaling

Prayer

Further Spiritual Reading, Reflection, Journaling, Prayer

Eucharist

Response: Thanksgiving, Offerings, Covenant

Returning to the World

Utilize the suggestions in the appendix or design your own plan for faithful living. Be sure to include times of regular review to help yourself maintain your walk with God.

Closing Prayer

Loving God, I offer open hands, open mind, open heart, and a willing spirit to hear continually your calling and sending voice. I abandon my life and ministry into your care with the assurance that you will lead me in paths of righteousness and goodness. *Amen.*

6.
WHO REALLY CALLS
AND SENDS?

*I*n my tradition pastors are appointed by a bishop, even when the place of ministry is a hospital, agency, or mission field. For more than forty years I have been under the appointment of a bishop and have accepted that appointment as God's call for me.

As a bishop of the church I have made well over one thousand appointments. Each of them involved a pastor and a congregation or employing agency. In some cases the pastor was reluctant and in some cases the congregation was reluctant. In other cases there was great anticipation and eagerness on the part of receiving institution, pastor, and family. In every case the appointment involved the lives of countless persons in significant and sometimes dramatic ways. Pastors and their families were uprooted from familiar settings and placed in strange surroundings to begin ministry anew and once again establish roots and relationships in their new community.

Congregations also experience stress as they say farewell to a pastor who has led them in their quest for faithful discipleship and as they seek to welcome a new representative of Christ in their midst.

Ideally, all appointments are made out of a prayerful, faithful, informed, and committed community. Whether that happens to be bishop and cabinet, call committee, or some other committee charged with the responsibility of calling and sending pastors, the goal is always that of matching the gifts for ministry of a given pastor with the needs and opportunities or mission of the congregation or parish. On more than one occasion in my experience, pastors and congregations questioned whether the appointment reflected God's call or some other and less significant voice. The questions are always valid and the answers can only be found in a faithful heart and in the midst of a prayerful and faithful community. Whether pastors respond to a congregation or committee's invitation or call or to a bishop's appointment, the question still arises, "From whence did this call come and who is sending me to this place of ministry?"

Daniel Biles, in his book *Pursuing Excellence in Ministry,* asserts that "it is only when one sees oneself as under a bone-deep sense of divine call to ministry that one can have a vision of one's own ministry and communicate that to one's congregation." Historically Christians have believed that it was God who called persons to ministry and it was obedience to that call which led persons to commitment to ministry. Christians have believed since the beginning that the pastoral office was divinely instituted. Thus, the validity, the legitimacy, and even fruitfulness of a pastor are not the result of his or her own invention. The call to ministry is not in the hands of a call committee or bishop but in the hands of God. The church is God's creation, and call to ministry within the church is God's call. All ministry flows out of the sending and sustaining activity of God. And all Christian response to a call to ministry is a response to God's call. It is such a sense of calling that permits persons to enter this demanding vocation. It is also this sense of calling that provides direction and strength to continue even when one is living out ministry in a "desert place."

A young woman facing ordination gave her bishop the following poem she had written:

> Dear Jesus, who did nothing of your own,
> but whatever came from God alone,
> when hands are laid upon my head
> bring to mind how you wept, and bled,
> and prayed the Father's will be done
> that in you, in him, we may be one.

Here is an ordinand facing ministry who clearly understands that ministry is a response to an invitation. An invitation that comes from outside oneself. An invitation that comes from God. While the urging may be experienced deep within, the call comes from beyond oneself. The response does rise up within us, but the call comes from outside ourselves. Here is an ordinand who wisely sees that the model for Christian ministry is Jesus, the selfless one, who gave himself fully and freely to God and to the ministry to which he had been sent.

She also saw that ministry is not without cost. Christian ministry is to follow the selfless way of Christ. To say that we are followers of Christ, representatives of Christ, servants of Christ, and to expect ease, comfort, and our own way is indeed an unthinkable contradiction.

To follow One who wept and bled, who prayed and struggled, who went to parties and weddings, who associated with saints and sinners, who was loved and embraced, who was misunderstood and doubted, who was revered and rejected, who was followed and betrayed, and who, in the eyes of the world, utterly failed, is to place oneself in the pathway of similar experiences. The disciple is not above the teacher. This is not to say that a pastor must live a life of unbearable experiences.

But it is to say that there is not only reward but also cost attached to the call to ministry in the name of Jesus Christ.

Shortly after I was consecrated a bishop I received a short letter from one of the pastors under my care. It was a young woman who wrote, "Be courageous and brave, your path will not be smooth. Be faithful for we need you and your faithfulness. Forget not that God is always with you. Shalom." Again, a young clergywoman knew deep within her, far beyond her years of experience, that wherever one seeks to live in faithfulness to Jesus Christ, the pathway will not always be smooth. She knew it would take courage to be a bishop or a deacon and to follow Christ in that vocation. And thus her admonition to me, one more than thirty years her senior in ministry, was an appropriate charge to be faithful. After all, that is our highest calling. To be faithful in the place where we are sent is never without its trial. To be faithful where we are sent is the ministry that leads to fruitfulness and now and then even to fulfillment.

Sometime later I received a letter from a pastor whose experience in ministry paralleled my own. In his letter he quotes from his own prayer journal for that day. "Save me from pettiness. Help me to keep my eyes fixed on Christ. Grant to me, O God, a humble use of mind and spirit to serve you with gladness. Lord, give me starch in my deepest self so that I may stand tall and strong for that which is noble, right, true, and Christlike." Later in his letter he says, "I wish my spiritual life were in better condition. If it were not for a clear memory of call to ministry it would be very difficult to continue on a day like this."

From all outward appearances this pastor has had an inordinately successful ministry. Wherever he has gone, the church has thrived and grown. The church under his leadership has grown in attendance, in mission outreach, in justice and evangelistic ministry, and in all of the standard indicators of evaluation. But perhaps even more importantly, wherever this pastor has served there has been a deeper growth, an immeasurable growth of commitment and faithfulness. Perhaps it was this immeasurable growth that has led to the growth in the standard indicators of evaluation—others were more rooted in God under this pastor's leadership. And yet he expresses misgivings about his own spiritual life. There is an obvious desire to go further, to be more complete, more faithful, more committed, more able. In the midst of the demands of ministry, with an obvious deep quest for faithfulness, it was the memory of his call to ministry that kept this pastor steady and faithful. Countless others have testified that the memory and recurring call to their own ministry have kept them going in difficult and trying times, as well as in challenging and exhilarating times.

Of course, that call has come to each of us in different ways. Because

God is infinite, and you and I are unique, our call cannot be the same. Thus, the times and ways in which the light of that calls seems to dim are equally unique to our own lives, call, and setting for ministry. There are those times when the certainty that we have previously known is difficult to recapture. Every pastor will face days of uncertainty, inadequacy, the pain of hard questions that cannot be answered and even the embarrassment of knowing that ultimately we have only Jesus Christ to offer to a world that chooses to make its gods out of material things.

There are other times when the failures are so deep and so far-reaching that we must ask, "God, if you called me to ministry, why, why has it turned out this way?" There are still other times when our ministry exhausts us and when our energy and resources seem to be entirely depleted. Yes, these times come to most persons who are engaged in ministry.

But even in these difficult and dark times, we can rehearse again God's call to us, remembering how it is that God has led us to this day, reliving again those moments of decision and assurance that guided us to where we are. Such reflection often leads us to prayers of thanksgiving for God's sustaining grace and not infrequently to a renewed sense that the call does indeed continue. At that moment our sense of calling is fresh, new, and powerful once again. Our ministry seems challenging and our hearts grow strong and brave again, ready to go on because we have been reminded that it is God who has called us and who sends us into the ministry of every day. We are reminded that God has not forsaken us and that the God of grace and love, mercy and justice, of might and wisdom is the God who has called us and uses even our weaknesses to bring forth the purpose and reign of God in church and world.

As I grow older I am more and more convinced that it matters little where we serve or what titles follow or precede our name. The question always remains the same, "Have we been faithful to our call to the ministry of Christ?" In our vocation we are often put in places where we receive unwarranted accolades and almost as frequently, unwarranted critique and criticism. But our self-worth is not determined by our accolades and it is not diminished by our critics. Our self-worth is determined by our relationship to the living God who claims us as daughters and sons. And our contribution to the reign of this God is not measured by accolades or criticisms; rather it is found in the answer to the simple question, "Have we been faithful to our call to the ministry of Jesus Christ?" We will find the answer to that question only in our conversation, communion, and companionship with Jesus Christ. It is in that conversation, communion, and companionship that we learn day by day that place of ministry has little to do with faithfulness and that the evaluation that others bring to ministry, while helpful, can never replace the self-examination that we must do and the examination that comes in intimacy with our faithful Savior.

Eugene Peterson laments that "American pastors are abandoning their posts left and right and at an alarming rate. They are not leaving their churches and getting other jobs. Congregations still pay their salaries. Their names remain on the church stationery and they continue to appear in pulpits on Sundays. But they are abandoning their posts, their calling." Peterson is correct in gleaning from the masters the secret of effective and faithful ministry. He identifies "a trained attentiveness to God in prayer, in scripture reading, in spiritual direction." His insistence that pastoral ministry has no integrity unless it is rooted in such attentiveness is in keeping with twenty centuries of pastoral experience. And to neglect this attentiveness to God is often to lose sight of our calling and to find ourselves simply going through the acts of ministry as if we were on cruise control, without careful, prayerful, and reflective attention to God or our calling.

This time apart is designed to resource your desire to be attentive to God. Out of such attentiveness we hear anew the call of God and realize afresh that however the call came to us, it first passed through the hands of God. Such knowledge is a gift of faith and it offers meaning, hope, and reward for a lifetime of ministry.

SPIRITUAL  READINGS

— SINGLED OUT —

Paul Minear uses the example of a drama to illustrate the meaning of a call. I paraphrase his idea this way: You are at the theater with a group of friends, sitting in a box; you are absorbed as a spectator of the drama taking place on the stage in front of you. Suddenly the author and director of the play steps out from the wings and, while the drama continues, shouts your name. "Joe Smith!" he calls. "Come here to the stage and get into the act; I have a part for you." The peculiar thing is, no one else hears him shout your name, and no one else moves or looks at you, for everyone is intently following the action on stage. Now you are aroused. You are embarrassed to leave your friends without a sensible explanation, but there is no logical reason for entering the drama except the compulsion from within. You begin to feel a panic, perhaps a cold sweat. What will you do? Will you suppress this urge to get into the play? Will you argue with the director? Will you leave the theater? Will you get up and throw yourself into the drama and try to influence the course of action according to the impulse that urges itself upon you?

This sense of being singled out, or of being called, is highly personal. There is no explanation as to why one is selected. If the action required is dangerous or disruptive of our normal routine, our automatic response is exactly like that of Moses: "Why me?" Yet the event so changes the situation in which we live that we feel either a compulsion to act or a need to explain to ourselves why we will not respond to the call. We find ourselves being pulled by an invisible power, and we are obliged to be attentive to what the power is coaching us to do.

—C. Ellis Nelson
How Faith Matures

— PREACHING THE TRUTH —

So the sermon hymn comes to a close with a somewhat unsteady amen, and the organist gestures the choir to sit down. Fresh from breakfast with his wife and children and a quick runthrough of the Sunday papers, the preacher climbs the steps to the pulpit with his sermon in hand. He hikes his black robe up at the knee so he will not trip over it on the way up. His mouth is a little dry. He has cut himself shaving. He feels as if he has swallowed an anchor. If it weren't for the honor of the thing, he would just as soon be somewhere else.

In the front pews the old ladies turn up their hearing aids, and a young lady slips her six-year-old a Lifesaver and a Magic Marker. A college sophomore home for vacation, who is there because he was dragged there, slumps forward with his chin in his hand. The vice-president of a bank who twice that week has seriously contemplated suicide places his hymnal in the rack. A pregnant girls feels the life stir inside her. A high-school math teacher, who for twenty years has managed to keep his homosexuality a secret for the most part even from himself, creases his order of service down the center with his thumbnail and tucks it under his knee. Pilate is there. The aqueduct man is there who has indicated that he will make it worth his while if his people get the contract, and Henry Ward Beecher is there. It is a busman's holiday for him. The vestry has urged him to take a week off for a badly needed rest, and he has come to hear how somebody else does it for a change. It is not that he doesn't love his wife, but just that, pushing sixty, he has been caught pre-posterously off-guard by someone who lets him open his heart to her, someone willing in her beauty to hear out the old spellbinder, who as a minister has never had anybody much to minister to him. King Lear is there with a bit of dried egg on his tie and weak kidneys.

The preacher pulls the little cord that turns on the lectern light and deals out his note cards like a riverboat gambler. The stakes have never been higher. Two minutes from now he may have lost his listeners completely to their own thoughts, but at this minute he has them in the palm of his hand. The silence in the shabby church is deafening because everybody is listening to it. Everybody is listening including even himself. Everybody knows the kind of things he has told them before and not told them, but who knows what this time, out of the silence, he will tell them?

Let him tell them the truth. Before the Gospel is a word, it is silence. It is the silence of their own lives and of his life. It is life with the sound turned off so that for a moment or two you can experience it not in terms of the words you make it bearable by but for the unutterable mystery that it is. Let him say, "Be silent and know that I am God, saith the Lord" (Ps. 46:10). Be silent and know that even by my silence and absence I am known. Be silent and listen to the stones cry out.

Out of the silence let the only real news come, which is sad news before it is glad news and that is fairy tale last of all. The preacher is not brave enough to be literally silent for long, and since it is his calling to speak the truth with love, even if he were brave enough, he would not be silent for long because we are none of us very good at silence. It says too much. So let him use words, but, in addition to using them to explain, expound, exhort, let him use them to evoke, to set us dreaming as well as thinking, to use words as at their most prophetic and truthful, the prophets used them to stir in us memories and longings and intuitions that we starve for without knowing that we starve. Let him use words which do not only try to give answers to the questions that we ask or ought to ask but which help us to hear the questions that we do not have words for asking and to hear the silence that those questions rise out of and the silence that is the answer to those questions. Drawing on nothing fancier than the poetry of his own life, let him use words and images that help make the surface of our lives transparent to the truth that lies deep within them, which is the wordless truth of who we are and who God is and the Gospel of our meeting.

—Frederick Buechner
Telling the Truth

— THE MESSINESS OF MINISTRY —

They asked Jesus, "Show us the Father." And in response, he portrayed a messy, divine recklessness at the very heart of reality:

A farmer went out to sow and he . . . carefully prepared the soil, removing all rocks and weeds, marking off neat rows, placing each seed exactly six inches from the other, covering each with three-quarters of an inch of soil?

No. This sower just began slinging seed. Seed everywhere. Some fell on the path, some on rocks, some in weeds, and some, miraculously, fell on good soil, took root, and rendered harvest. That's what the Word of God is like, said Jesus.

A farmer (as I recall, it was the same farmer) had a field. The servants came running in breathlessly: "Master, there's weeds coming up in your new wheat."

"An enemy must have done this!" cries the farmer.

Enemy, my eye. You get this sort of agricultural mess when you sow seed with such abandon.

"Do you want us to go out and carefully root up those weeds from your good wheat?" asked the servants.

"No, let 'em grow. I just love to see stuff grow. We'll sort it all out in September."

And Jesus said, "That's God's kingdom."

In his commentary on these parables, Calvin sees clearly that they are meant for clergy, concluding his interpretation by warning that it is vain to seek a church free from every spot.

Aquinas spoke of the "divine economy," and that's fine provided we understand that it is exorbitant economics for a woman who would tear her living room apart until she found her stray quarter, a father who plows ten grand into a welcome-home party for a prodigal, a shepherd called "good" for his willingness to lay down his life for a $3.95-plus-postage sheep.

Forsake all thinking that is categorical; let go all theology that presumes to be systematic, but is an affront to the way this God runs a farm. . . .

"Point us to the kingdom," they asked Jesus. And he replied, "A man gave a feast, spared no expense, got the best caterers in town, hired a band, sent out invitations to all his friends and cronies, and they began to make excuses." They are busy, cleaning out the garage, sorting their socks. They refuse.

And the Lord of the banquet gets real mad. So he sends out his servants a second time, telling them to bring in the poor, the maimed, the blind, the lame—in short, those with nothing to do on a Saturday night. And they came.

And Jesus says the kingdom of God is like that. God's idea of church is a party with people you wouldn't be caught dead with on a Saturday night.

Just when I get my church all sorted out, sheep from the goats, saved from the damned, hopeless from the hopeful, somebody makes a move, gets out of focus, cuts loose, and I see why Jesus never wrote systematic theology.

Just when I settle down to keep house in the church, just me and my flock, Jesus says, "By the way, I have other sheep, who are not of this fold. I'm going to find them too" (Jn 10:16).

So you and I can give thanks that the locus of Christian thinking appears to be shifting from North America and Northern Europe where people write rules and obey them, to places like Africa and Latin America where people still know how to dance.

And I think it's wonderful that most of you have spent time learning Greek, a marvelously *useless* language. You can't use Greek to build a "mega church," nor will it fold out into a bed. We make you learn Greek (now the truth can be told) not because knowing Greek has anything to do with successful Christian ministry, but in the hope that we will thereby render you so impractical that, having wasted so much time with a dead language, you may not balk at wasting an afternoon with an eighty-year-old nursing-home resident, or spending a Saturday listening to the life of a troubled teenager, or taking hours to write a sermon that no more than twenty will ever hear. . . . You can't be a pastor and be neat.

"She could have gone to law school. Best undergraduate I ever taught," he said, as we veered off the main highway and made our way down a narrow country road in West Virginia. We pulled before the little white frame Presbyterian church, with the sign hanging from a rusted chain, peeling paint, with the name of the church and, underneath, painted poorly, "The Rev. Julie Jones—Pastor."

And my friend said, "Damn, what a waste."

But the reckless farmer who slung the seed and the woman who pulled up her carpet and moved the living room furniture into the yard in pursuit of her lost quarter, the giver of the banquet for the forgotten, and the shepherd who threw away his life for the sheep, laughed with disordered gospel delight.

—William H. Willimon
The Princeton Seminary Bulletin

— MOVING ON —

Word drifts back that an old friend in a former church has died. It is years since we last saw each other. But we were close when I was there. It is the way of being a pastor. You come, you go. Then suddenly you are back, as with this letter about my friend. He was on the committee that "called" me.

Moving on is perhaps the single hardest thing about the ministry. You get close over the years, and then it is time to move on. One wonders about the sense of that. Why do ministers "have to move on"? Doctors don't. Lawyers don't. Accountants don't. They build up a practice. They stay. It would be economic suicide to go.

We are here now. I see no reason to go. We have been here several years. In many denominations that would mean "time to move on." But such conventional thinking fails to consider the advantages of staying. To be sure, there are disadvantages. One wears out one's welcome with certain people; for some, one begins to abrade. Others feel the congregation needs a fresh face.

But the advantages far outweigh. We are close now. We are a family. One does not break up a family because the pay is better and the challenge greater. The challenge is not necessarily greater. It would take another several years to get this close to another congregation; and if the church were twice the size of this one, it would take twice as long. What is the point?

It takes a while to learn what should be obvious from the start. One does not always know where home is in one's first parish or even one's second. One is looking ahead to the next call. But by the time of the third or fourth parish, one becomes unconventionally wise. These are your people, your parish. This is where you were meant to be. The people on the committee that called you have become some of the most important people in your life.

So when the letter came about my old friend on the old committee, I looked back with affection. He took me to the airplane through the snow. He chaired the committee on worship. He and his wife took us to the ball park. They had us over. Now he is gone. I dropped her a note and thought, "What a paltry thing, a note, to say to her all I could have said to him while I was there." I hope he knew.

—Robert K. Hudnut
This People, This Parish

— THE SELFLESS WAY OF CHRIST —

Something which existed since the beginning, that we have heard and we have seen with our own eyes; that we have watched and touched with our hands; the Word, who is life—this is our subject.

(1 John 1:1)

As no other words in the New Testament, these words make clear that our ministerial vocation emerges out of an experience that involves our whole being. The subject of our ministry is Jesus Christ, the Word who was from the beginning with God and was made flesh to live among us (cf. John 1:1, 14). To be a minister is to witness to this Word, to reveal the presence of this Word within us as well as among us. Yet, this witness, which takes the form of preaching and teaching, of celebrating and counseling, of organizing and struggling to alleviate the suffering of our fellow human beings, is a true witness only when it emerges out of a genuine personal encounter, a true experience of love. We can only call ourselves witnesses of Jesus Christ when we have heard him with our own ears, seen him with our own eyes, and touched him with our own hands.

The basis of the mission of the 12 apostles was not their knowledge, training, or character, but their having lived with Jesus. Paul, who was not with Jesus while he was traveling with his disciples, encountered him on the road to Damascus. This experience was the foundation on which all his apostolic work was built.

There has never been a minister whose influence has not been directly related to a personal and intimate experience of the Lord. This deep and personal encounter can take as many forms and shapes as there are people, cultures, and ages. Ignatius of Antioch, Anthony of the Desert, Gregory the Great, Benedict, Bernard and Francis, Ignatius of Loyola, Theresa of Avila, John of the Cross, Martin Luther, John Wesley, John Fox and John Bunyan, Charles de Foucauld, Dag Hammarskjold, Martin Luther King, Jr., Thomas Merton, Jean Vanier, Mother Teresa, Dorothy Day—all these witnesses have seen the Lord, and their actions and words emerge from that vision.

Thus, ministry and the spiritual life belong together. Living a spiritual life is living in an uninterrupted and intimate communion with the Lord. It is seeing, hearing, and touching. Living a life of ministry is witnessing to him in the midst of this world. It is opening the eyes of our brothers and sisters in the human family to his presence among us, so that they too may enter into this relationship of love.

When our ministry does not emerge from a personal encounter, it quickly becomes a tiring routine and a boring job. On the other hand, when our spiritual life no longer leads to an active ministry, it quickly degenerates into introspection and self-scrutiny, and thus loses its dynamism. Our life in Christ and our ministry in his name belong together as the two beams of the cross. . . .

The Spiritual Life

If discipleship requires following Jesus in downward mobility, is this truly a human option? Is it possible to take Jesus totally seriously? Or would that simply mean embarking on a self-destructive, even masochistic, road? I wonder if in practice we haven't already answered this question. Haven't we already decided that Jesus cannot be taken at his word, but rather needs to be adapted to our upwardly mobile way?

I am not asking this as a cynic or a moralist. That would not be taking the matter seriously. Rather, I want to raise the question concerning the nature of the spiritual life. When we think that living the downward way is within our reach and that our task is simply to imitate Christ, we have misunderstood the basic truth which has been revealed to us.

The downward way is God's way, not ours. God reveals himself as God to us in the downward pull, because only he who is God can empty himself of his divine privileges and become as we are. The great mystery upon which our faith rests is that the One who is in no way like us, who cannot be compared with us, nor enter into competition with us, has descended among us and taken on our mortal flesh.

This downward mobility is unnatural for us, because it belongs to the essence of our sinful, broken condition that every fiber of our being is tainted by rivalry and competition. We are always finding ourselves, even against our own best desires and judgments, on the familiar road of upward mobility. The moment we think we are humble, we discover that we are wondering if we are more humble than our neighbor and that we already have some type of reward in the back of our mind.

Downward mobility is the divine way, the way of the cross, the way of Christ. It is precisely this divine way of living that our Lord wants to give to us through his Spirit. How the way of the Spirit radically differs from the way of the world is made clear in the words of the apostle Paul to the Christians of Corinth:

> The hidden wisdom of God . . . is the wisdom that none of the masters of this age have ever known. . . . We teach . . . the things that no eye has seen and no ear has heard, things beyond the mind of man. . . . These are the very things that God has revealed to us through the Spirit, for the Spirit reaches the depths of everything, the depths of God. . . . Now instead of the spirit of the world, we have received the Spirit that comes from God, to teach us to understand the gifts that he has given us. Therefore we teach . . . in the way the Spirit teaches us: we teach spiritual things spiritually. (1 Corinthians 2:7-13)

These words summarize succinctly the meaning of the spiritual life. They tell us that it is the life in which the Spirit of Christ, who reaches the depths of God, is given to us so that we may know, with a new knowledge of mind and heart, the way of God.

When Jesus died on the cross, the disciples experienced a deep sense of loss and failure. They thought it was all over and clung to each other in the fear that they would be dealt with as Jesus had been. They had not understood the downward way of God. But when, on the day of Pentecost, the Spirit whom Jesus had promised came, everything changed. The Spirit blew their fears away. The Spirit made them see who Jesus truly was, and revealed to them the new way. The Spirit gave them the strength to proclaim to all nations the way of the cross, the downward way, as the way to salvation.

Jesus himself tells us who the Spirit is. On the evening before his death he said to his disciples:

> It is for your own good that I am going, because unless I go, the Advocate [the Spirit] will not come to you; but if I do go, I will send him to you. And . . . he will lead you to the complete truth, since he will not be speaking as from himself but will only say what he has learned . . . all he tells you will be taken from what is mine. Everything the Father has is mine; that is why I said, "All he tells you will be taken from what is mine." (John 16:7-15)

Here Jesus reveals to us that the Spirit is the fullness of God's being. It is the fullness that Jesus calls "the truth." When Jesus says that the Spirit will lead us to the complete truth, he means that the Spirit will make us full participants in the divine life, a life that makes us into new people, living with a new mind and in a new time: the mind and time of Jesus Christ.

In and through the Spirit of Christ, we become those who are Christs living in all places and at all times. In and through the Spirit, we come to know all that Jesus knew, and we are able to do all that he did. This is the great wisdom of God, the wisdom that none of the masters of this age have ever known, the wisdom which has remained hidden from the learned and the clever but has been revealed to mere children, the wisdom which comes to us through the Spirit and can only be taught to us spiritually.

Thus discipleship is the life of the Spirit in us, by whom we are lifted up into the divine life itself and receive new eyes to see, new ears to hear, and new hands to touch. Being lifted up in God's own life, we are sent into the world to witness to what we have seen with our own eyes, have heard with our own ears, and have touched with our own hands. It is a witness to the life of God's word in us.

The way of the cross, the downward mobility of God, becomes our way not because we try to imitate Jesus, but because we are transformed into living Christs by his Spirit. The spiritual life is the life of the Spirit of Christ in us, a life that sets us free to be strong while weak, to be free while captive, to be joyful while in pain, to be rich while poor, to be on the downward way of salvation while living in the midst of an upwardly mobile society.

Although this spiritual life might seem enigmatic, intangible, and elusive to us who belong to a scientific age, its fruits leave little doubt about the radical transformation it brings about. Love, joy, peace, patience, kindness, goodness, trustfulness, gentleness, and self-control are indeed the qualities of our Lord himself and reveal his presence in the midst of a world so torn apart by idolatry, envy, greed, sexual irresponsibility, war, and other sin (see Galatians 5:19-23). It is not hard to distinguish the upward pull of our world from the downward pull of Christ.

—Henri Nouwen
Sojourners

— THE CALL TO THE MISSION OF MINISTRY —

Experiencing the call of God has always been at the heart of Christian understandings of the missional character of the church's ministry. . . .

Apostles served as ambassadors, persons who were called and "sent out" to serve and share the gospel. A missional ministry is a calling, not a career. Literally, ministry means "to serve." Thus it is not just another job, occupation, or profession but a vocation one accepts in response to a summons from a loving God. The church needs a laity and clergy who are willing to think, live, and die the life of an apostle of Jesus Christ. According to Bishop Dan E. Solomon, the church requires a "leadership that is missional and not just functional."

The call came to Moses while he was doing the respectable thing, minding his own business, leading an ordinary shepherd's life, tending to his in-law's sheep in the obscurity of the wilderness. Imagine his surprise and his shock as he confronted a burning bush and an angel appeared. He must have wondered if he was hallucinating, or if he had been sucking for too long on a strange weed! But in a response to the call, "Moses, Moses!" he responded, saying "Here I am" (Exodus 3:4).

Skeptics might question whether the event at the burning bush ever took place. After all, no independent on-site verifications occurred, no secondary witnesses testified, and no scientific observations of flaming plants existed. What we do have, however, is the faith history of the Hebrew people, who never questioned the reality that God spoke to a simple shepherd, commissioned him to be their prophetic leader, and subsequently led them out of the oppression of the Egyptians into the promised land. Neither do we have any evidence that Moses ever doubted he had been duly called by the Divine, nor that God accompanied him in his missional ministry no matter how deep the difficulty or torturous the trial.

The fiery drama of Moses' call contrasts with the biblical account of how Jesus recruited his first disciples. Passing the corner of Market and Main, along the Sea of Galilee, Jesus saw some ordinary fishermen named Simon Peter and Andrew. He said to them, "Follow me, and I will make you fish for people." No questions asked! No requests for a job description or a personnel handbook! Why, not even an explanation of the pension plan! Instead Scripture simply says: "Immediately they left their nets and followed him." A short distance away, perhaps at the corner of Sin and Decadence, Jesus again stopped and seeing the son of Zebedee, and John, his brother, called to them, asking that they quit mending their nets and join in a different type of fishing expedition. No blazing bushes! No angelic voices! Just the authoritative call to adventure in the mission of ministry (Matthew 4:18-22).

Since the time when Jesus called the earliest disciples to drop their work and follow him, the church has asked of its leadership the nature and meaning of their call. For Paul, the decision to enter the ministry was not a choice among professions but a response to God's command on the Damascus road. Saul had a career, Paul had a calling. That call motivated, sustained, and empowered Paul in his missionary travels, despite persecution, imprisonment, controversy, and setbacks.

The call comes to laity and clergy, sometimes for a lifetime of full-time professional church work, sometimes for lay vocational service in the world. God calls persons, not just into the priesthood but into all of life's noble vocations and avocations. The dominant biblical understanding of the idea of calling is an urgent invitation or summons from God to enter into a life of service. Martin Luther emphasized that every vocation was sacred; we can make out of any work a calling of honor to God. Johann Sebastian Bach wrote the initials—S.D.G., *Soli Deo Gloria*, "to the glory of God alone" and J. J., *Jesu juva*, "Help me, Jesus"—at the top of each composition he wrote. The vocation of every man and woman, noted Albert Schweitzer, is to serve other people.

The summons to Moses, the invitation of Jesus, and the rugby player's call to Hersey's father represent but a handful of illustrations. God's call can be traced through the Scriptures from the experience of Abraham and Jeremiah to Mary and Paul. It can be substantiated in history with the call experienced by Augustine or John Wesley or Martin Luther King, Jr., or Mother Teresa. In addition, consider the individual stories of Christians who over the centuries have quietly lived out their lives in humble service, and we can see that the church universal truly connotes a community of the called.

God's request often requires a struggle of the soul, since the divine command may be contrary to our human desire for comfort, success, and wealth. In John Wesley's terms, accepting the call means being "ready to do anything, to lose anything, to suffer anything." No wonder we often pretend not to hear!

Sometimes people misunderstand what God tries to tell them. There is an old story about a farmer who thought he had received a call to be ordained because he had seen in the clouds the letters "P C," which he interpreted to mean, "preach Christ." After many frustrating and fumbling attempts to preach, he realized he was really called to "plow corn." Today God calls persons not only to "preach Christ" but to "program computers" and to do "professional counseling."

God's call to mission and ministry comes in many different ways and at various times. It may be as dramatic as a burning bush to a shepherd, or as dynamic as the invitation of Jesus to some fishing folk, or as dry as the quiet words of a rugby player to a college student. When one experiences the call, and responds, inevitably lives change and history is transformed. The status quo is upset and revolutions are unleashed.

One significant phenomenon currently is that so many second-career persons are leaving the security of their secular professions to become Christian pastors. Lawyers are walking away from lucrative careers.

Clinical psychologists are training to be preachers. Journalists are choosing to proclaim the Word. Homemakers are discovering there is life and ministry after age forty! Seminaries now attract mature Christian persons who come to offer the church and humanity insights from their rich life experiences and knowledge. A similar phenomenon also occurs in reverse, with persons moving away from ordained ministries and taking on the yoke of service inherent in business and professional vocations.

Everyone can be a vessel of God's loving and liberating mission in the world. God needs business persons willing to commit their lives to integrity and public service. God needs professionals ready to serve not only individual human needs but also to ensure that their professions meet the highest ethical standards. God needs students willing to surrender their lives to the full-time service of church and humanity. Whatever the circumstances of life, God has a calling for the mission of ministry. A person confined to bed in a nursing home can still write letters on behalf of Amnesty International to protest torture and other global violations of human rights. The manifold possibilities for fighting world hunger and the madness of the arms race exist. God calls people to tasks, both great and small, long-term and of shorter duration.

A sixty-year-old man who recently accompanied a short-term volunteer mission team to the South Pacific illustrates what one person can accomplish. He had been affiliated with the church primarily because he thought it was good for his wife and children.

In Tonga he visited a boys' school that owned a herd of cows to provide milk for the students and to provide revenue to support the school. In the course of conversation, he learned about the school's erractic electrical supply, which often failed at milking time. An electrical engineer by profession, he naturally asked, "Well, why don't you get a standby generator?" The director of the school replied that they had had one for twenty years "but nobody knows how to make it work."

Early the next morning, after a sleepless night, he knocked on the mission leader's door and announced he was going back to the school to fix their generator. She replied, "Well, Brother, the Holy Spirit has got ahold of you. You are being called to fix that generator."

He decided to take another month off from his business to return to Tonga, where with the help of the students, he built a platform for the generator and got it working. His postcard back home read: "August 3— 6:30 P.M. Engine started."

Local newspapers reported the event and the King and Queen of Tonga visited the site. What had happened to this man, however, proved more significant: for the first time in his life he knew what it meant to serve other people in the name of Jesus Christ. Recently he reported his plans to return to Tonga, saying, "They have another job for me to do."

God has many engines that need to be restarted in this world, if the divine vision of justice, peace, and the integrity of creation is to be realized. If we allow the Holy Spirit to teach us, we can each find a calling for our talents and resources. The call for the mission of ministry is for new Christian apostles in a nuclear, global, and ecological age. Needed are more respondents saying "Here am I. Send me."

—Donald E. Messer
A Conspiracy of Goodness

— MINISTRY AND THE YOKE OF OBEDIENCE —

Franz Hildebrandt once observed that his reading of the New Testament convinced him that the picture of a minister of the gospel is not so much a person "in orders" as a person "under orders." Hildebrandt was a good Methodist. As this book has suggested, Methodism's theology of ordination is concerned less with the matter of the validity of ministerial orders and more with the obligation of the ordained to be "under orders" for the gospel and church of Jesus Christ.

Being "under orders" means that one is obedient and accountable. Calvin insisted that one who is ordained must understand that "he is no longer a law unto himself, but bound in servitude to God and the church." The language of service, bonds, orders, and obedience is not compatible with secular, liberal, twentieth-century America. We do not like to admit to any limitations of individual freedom. But the Christian gospel challenges us because we are confronted by Jesus himself who, "though he was in the form of God, did not count equality with God a thing to be grasped, but emptied himself, taking the form of a servant, being born in human likeness. And being found in human form he humbled himself and became obedient unto death, even death on a cross" (Phil. 2:6-8).

Ordained ministers are called to representative self-emptying lives of obedience and service. The greatest potential for renewal in ministry is for the ordained to reaffirm their high calling to live "under orders." Let John Wesley's prayer be our own:

> We take upon ourselves with joy the yoke of obedience. We are no longer our own, but thine. Put us to what thou wilt. Rank us with whom thou wilt. Put us to doing. Put us to suffering. Let us be employed for thee or laid aside for thee, exalted for thee or brought low for thee. Let us

be full. Let us be empty. Let us have all things. Let us have nothing. We freely and heartily yield all things to thy pleasure and disposal.

—Dennis M. Campbell
The Yoke of Obedience

— SUCH A TIME AS THIS —

Breaking into our individual and collective emotions and expectations we hear the voice of Mordecai, once addressed to Esther, now speaking to us, "Who knows whether you have not come to the kingdom for such a time as this?" In Mordecai's question we are reminded of the heart of our Jewish and Christian heritage—a heritage that believes that our lives are guided by divine purpose rather than by chance or fate. Although the book of Esther has the unusual distinction of never mentioning the name of God, it is clear that its author had a keen sense of the divine timeliness of events. Esther had not become queen at that time and place by some random act of fate. Esther was where she was for a purpose.

Through an unusual twist of events Esther had become Jewish queen of this predominantly Gentile nation. When Haman (one of the king's advisors) won permission from the king to destroy all the Jews in the country, Mordecai (Esther's cousin and guardian) knew that Esther was the only one in the kingdom who could persuade her husband, the king, to undo Haman's plan. And so he beseeched her: "If you keep silence at such a time as this, relief and deliverance will rise for the Jews from another quarter, but you and your father's house will perish. And who knows whether you have not come to the kingdom for such a time as this?" Mordecai knew that Esther was where she was for a reason; her life had purpose.

As we who are here standing at the threshold of a new year hear Mordecai's word to Esther, we know it is a word to us as well, for it coincides with the Christian understanding of divine providence which tells us that we are where we are for a purpose. We have not just been thrown together into this place by a random act of fate; rather, for such a time as this, we have been called for a purpose. Our understanding of divine providence says to each of us, "You are here for a reason, and your being here makes a difference."

"Who knows whether you have not come to the kingdom for such a time as this?" If you think those words spoken to us are not as urgent as when they were spoken to Esther, think again. We gather at a time when the Presbyterian Church and many other denominations are experiencing an unprecedented decline. Could it be that genuine renewal of the church will occur only when we recapture the church's distinct identity in the world through critical and sympathetic understanding of the history of our faith, through a renewed ability to read the Bible with discernment, teach and preach with passion, counsel with compassion, and stand against the powers and principalities of the world with courage? In short, could it be that renewal in the church in part begins with mastering all those things taught in seminary? While the renewal of the church does not fall on your shoulders alone, who knows whether you were not called into the kingdom for such a time as this? Your life has purpose, and your being here makes a difference.

If you think Mordecai's words are not as urgent now as when they were spoken to Esther, think again. We gather today one week from the 28th anniversary of the death of four little girls who were killed when a bomb was thrown into the 16th Street Baptist Church in Birmingham, Alabama. Could it be that almost three decades later, we are called to honor *their* memory and *our* baptism by seeking to mend the divisions which exist even in our church among the races, among different nationalities, and between men and women? While reconciliation among peoples does not fall on your shoulders alone, who knows whether you were not called into the kingdom for such a time as this? Your life has purpose, and your being here makes a difference.

One of the most important tasks facing us lies in discerning the purpose for which God has called us to this time and to this place. Perhaps it is easy to accept the urgency and challenge of Mordecai's words standing as we are with great resolve at the beginning of the year. Experience tells us, however, that the everydayness of our routine will dull that sense of urgency. Those books that seemed so exciting sitting on our shelf can be tedious when we actually sit down to read them. Our commitment to urgent issues of the day can wane from the lack of energy that comes with busy schedules. Furthermore, it isn't just the everydayness of life, but also the sudden tragedies of life, that can leave us without direction. What do we do when our conviction is overcome by cowardice, our sense of purpose by a sense of futility, our faith by doubt? What then of divine providence? How then do we fulfill the purpose to which we have been called?

If in the days to come your doubt becomes stronger than your hope, and the burden of life bigger than its sense of purpose, and failure seems to loom larger than success, then remember the image of Peter.

I have often heard people who are in the midst of radical doubt say: "If I could just see a miracle, I could believe." Peter is proof that this isn't necessarily true. Peter is right in the middle of a miracle. He is *walking on water*. The miraculous is happening to him, happening all around him. What does Peter do? He doubts. Right in the very midst of a miracle Peter's faith falters. Seeing the wind, he is afraid and begins to sink and so calls out, "Lord save me!" What follows is one of the most comforting passages of Scripture. The very next words after Peter's cry of fear and doubt are: "Jesus *immediately* reached out his hand and caught him."

God does not demand of us what we cannot do. We are never called to a purpose in life bigger than we can manage. When you cannot bear the purpose for which you were called into the world, when you are more depressed than hopeful, and feeling more left out than included, the grace of God reaches out, catches hold of you, and will never let you go. As you come to the communion table and then go forth into this new year keep in mind two affirmations of the Christian faith: (1) Your life has purpose; your being here makes a difference. (2) In your highest hopes and lowest failure, the love of God sustains you.

In breaking bread remember that Jesus the Messiah, who lived and died for this world, upholds you with a love that will not let you go. In drinking from the cup remember that your cup, your portion in life, involves the covenantal promise to live in the world as people who recognize the purpose to which God has called them. And as often as you eat this bread and drink this cup, you proclaim the Lord's death—*you* proclaim the Lord's death—until he comes. And it *is* for such a time as this that you have come into the kingdom.

—Nancy J. Duff
The Princeton Seminary Bulletin

Since we cannot make the journey backward into
    innocence,
  help us go forward into wisdom.
Since we cannot begin again from the beginning,
  help us to go on faithfully from here.
Since we cannot turn ourselves by our own willing,
  do thou turn us toward thee.
Amen.

—Edward Tyler
Prayers in Celebration of the Turning Year

APPENDIX:
RETURNING TO THE WORLD

The story of Perpetua, one of the early Christian martyrs, who lived from 181 to 203 is a beautiful story of fidelity. In spite of every conceivable temptation and pressure, she remained faithful. Her relationship to the living Christ was so vital and strong that infidelity became an impossibility for her even when the cost of fidelity was her life.

While I am moved and inspired by the life of Perpetua, I recognize that sometimes the enormous test, such as the one she faced, is easier to deal with than the relentless and subtle erosion caused by trivial temptations and barely perceptible variations from our true course of fidelity to God. A thousand minor decisions can turn our lives away from the light of Christ until we are, at best, a dim reflection. Therefore, it is essential for clergy to build into their daily and weekly schedules those times when life and vocation can be refocused and more accurately tuned to be in harmony with our Creator God.

I have found that there are some essential tools that can help us in this returning and refocusing process. They are spiritual disciplines fashioned over the centuries and handed down to us by those who have made this journey. You have probably practiced some of these disciplines before, but I encourage you to utilize them fully and build them into your own pattern of life until they become "automatic tuning devices" for you. The number of disciplines is large and not all of them may be appropriate for you. It seems to me that some disciplines are essential if we are to live our lives in fidelity to the One who made us, calls us, sends us, and sustains us. Included in the short list of essentials are: 1) daily reading and reflection, 2) some act of compassion and witness, 3) the practice of prayer and prayerful living, 4) corporate worship, and 5) life within some covenant community or small group for support and direction. These are the essentials that you will want to include in your pattern of life.

It is in the practice of these disciplines that we meet Jesus more fully and develop more completely our relationship with him. It is in Jesus that we see most clearly the image of God which we seek to reflect more clearly. It is in our relationship to Jesus that we recognize true fidelity and experience God's call to us for a covenental relationship—a relationship marked by fidelity, a relationship marked by God's presence and participation in our lives. Susanne Johnson (*Spiritual Formation in the Classroom*) is correct in saying that "one cannot become Christian without learning to pray, to confess and repent, to search the Scriptures, or to seek justice for the socially cast off." For it is in our searching of the Scriptures, our life of prayer, our compassion and justice, and our confession and repentance, that we begin to see more clearly the image of Jesus Christ. And it is only when we see that image clearly that we are in a position to incorporate Christ within our lives.

A PATTERN FOR LIFE

Days apart end and we return to the demands of daily ministry that call for our attention. Our experience is not unlike that of the disciples who were sent out on a challenging and unencumbered ministry as recorded in the sixth chapter of the Gospel of Mark. When they returned they reported what they had experienced and Jesus, recognizing their need for nurture and renewal, invites them to the desert for rest and reflection. A similar invitation has resulted in this time apart for you.

But now the time has come to re-enter your active ministry in the world. Mark's gospel says Jesus had compassion on the multitudes because they were like sheep without a shepherd and, almost at once, this compassion led them back into the ministry of teaching and feeding the crowds. Soon your own pastoral instincts and compassion will not let you go and soon you will be actively engaged in your ministry of shepherding, following the model that the Good Shepherd provides for us all. But how will you stay in touch with that Good Shepherd? How will you stay attached to the vine? How will you stay connected to the Source of Life Abundant in the midst of your ministry? How will you receive the Water of Life to refresh your own soul as you seek to bring refreshment to the souls in your care?

Many persons have found that developing a pattern of life is a process that can keep them in touch with God's sustaining grace for a lifetime of ministry. Such a pattern of life will be uniquely fitted to your personal needs and gifts as well as the context in which you are practicing ministry. This pattern of life can be simple or complex and is designed to provide structure, guidance, and sustenance in your walk with Jesus Christ as a Christian minister. From the beginning Christianity has sought to identify those practices that help the followers of Jesus to live faithfully in a broken world. These practices became rules and were available in written form as early as 346 (Pachomius). Within monasticism, a rule of life is an accepted and expected way of bringing form and structure to a faithful life of discipleship. Outside of monasticism, a way of life or pattern of life is also widely practiced as a part of discipleship. Since the first century, Christians have practiced a variety of disciplines to assist them in becoming and remaining faithful disciples.

What follows is a simple pattern of life to give guidance as you develop your own way of living in companionship with the living Christ. The pattern will likely grow and change as you grow and change, but following such a pattern can keep you aware of and attentive to the One who calls, sends and sustains you in ministry.

As you complete a day apart on retreat, create your own plan as you return to the world of active ministry. This day that you are completing has had some structure as well as great flexibility and freedom. The structure of the day was designed to keep you attentive to God and open to God's activity in your life. But what about tomorrow? What will tomorrow look like for you? The answer to these questions will provide first steps in the development of a pattern of life that can bring nurture, guidance, and companionship to you for the rest of your life. A simple and easy way to begin this development is to answer the question, "How will I be attentive and responsive to God all day long, every day, every week, every month and every year? What will be included in my pattern of life?

Read the suggestions included for a daily, weekly, monthly, and annual pattern of life. After you have done so, take time to list the items that you want to include in your own plan for faithful living. Once you have determined through prayer and discernment which items should be included in your pattern of life, begin to list them in this fourfold pattern of daily, weekly, monthly, and annual practices.

A DAILY PATTERN

A daily pattern of life may include some or all of the items listed below. Again I want to underscore that a pattern for life must be your own. Including something that may be right for a friend does not make it right for you. On the other hand, be willing to risk a new venture and a new discipline in your life and ministry. Prayerfully and thoughtfully consider your own unique spiritual journey, the context and nature of your ministry, and then select those items that seem to hold special promise for your own spiritual nurture and growth.

First determine a sacred place and time that you will observe daily. It is an important first step in any pattern of life. I have found morning and a home study particularly helpful in my own spiritual life. However, if neither seem available or appropriate, find the best place and the best time for you. The time could be evening, midday or midnight. The important thing is to establish a sacred time when you will give undivided attention to your walk with God. The sacred place could be your home study, bedroom, a corner of the furnace room, the altar area of the church or a place in the woods. Wherever this sacred place is, let it become for you a place for worship, prayer, and dedication. Using a cross, icon, candle, or some other religious symbol can remind you of the sacredness of this place and be a constant invitation to your attentiveness to God.

For many this daily pattern is centered in some kind of daily office. *A Guide to Prayer for All God's People*, *The Book of Common Prayer*, and *A Guide to Prayer for Ministers and Other Servants* continue to be useful guides for many persons. You may choose to use one of these guides or some other resource, such as a daily service of prayer and praise or a daily office in your church's hymnbook or book of worship. These daily patterns include reflection on Scripture, prayer and response and can give structure to your daily time apart.

Each of us can benefit from other practices or helps throughout the day. Prayer, upon awakening, can be a wonderful beginning to a day of companionship with the living Christ. A religious symbol or a favorite text fastened to the mirror where you apply make-up or shave can be a helpful way of calling your attention to God's presence with you. Prayer at mealtimes is one of the ways of expressing gratitude for God's abundant and sustaining grace in your life. Prayer upon retiring gives an opportunity to review the day, confess failures, receive forgiveness, give thanks for expressions of grace, and recommit to faithful discipleship before one finally commends all of life into the care of God.

A weekly pattern of life simply includes each of the daily patterns for a week and then adds appropriate disciplines to that week's activity. John Wesley believed that acts of devotion, acts of compassion, and acts of witness were necessary means of grace for every Christian. You may wish to establish a way of incorporating at least two of these means of grace into your pattern of life every week. Or, you may determine at the beginning to include all three.

Many persons have found weekly Eucharist a marvelous source of God's grace. Some have discovered a congregation where the Eucharist is offered daily and where they are able to receive the sacrament from another pastor.

Perhaps the most important addition to your weekly pattern of life is the observance of the Sabbath. Pastors, as much or more than any, need a

Sabbath. So, before leaving this time of retreat and planning for a weekly pattern, add a Sabbath and write it into your calendar for the next six months. It will never be easier than it is today and it will always require discipline on your part.

A monthly pattern incorporates the daily and weekly patterns and adds those items that you consider essential to faithful discipleship. You might consider adding such things as a day apart, a day given in mission and ministry with and on behalf of the poor and marginalized. This could be a day in an AIDS ward, working in a transient shelter, working in a hospice or a hospital as a volunteer. Some have found that a day a month with Habitat for Humanity or some other organization building low cost housing is a wonderful means of grace that provides an abundance of nurture and sustenance for every participant. Others have found that reading at least one new book each month is a means of grace and a source of God's direction and inspiration.

Finally, incorporate your daily, weekly, and monthly patterns into an annual pattern of life and add items that you feel are needed to make your walk with God unique and complete. Scheduling an annual retreat of at least three days may be a place to begin. In the early days of the year find at least one day to review the past year, to read your journal, to contemplate the years events and activities, and to listen once again to each of these events and see how they have been an expression of God's will and purpose for your life. Review your pattern of life and make the changes you feel led to make as you enter the new year.

This may also be a good time to consider finding and working with a spiritual guide, a spiritual friend, or a covenant group. Relating to such spiritual companions often brings encouragement, hope, and direction. Finally, record on a blank calendar or on a sheet of paper those acts that you intend to incorporate into your own pattern for life. This calendar page or sheet of paper can be placed on your desk or in your Bible as a helpful reminder of your commitment to a faithful and sustaining walk with God.

Later you may want to prayerfully explore books such as Richard Foster's *Celebration of Discipline* or Dallas Willard's *Spirit of the Disciplines* to discover other disciplines to add to your pattern of life.

The daily pattern you have created can be a wonderful source of guidance and grace for your spiritual journey. Use it for at least a month before making major adjustments. Your next day apart will be a good time to review and adjust your pattern for life. A disciplined daily reflection on the Scriptures coupled with prayer and response will bring rich rewards to those who fashion such a pattern of life. Further, this kind of faithful companionship with the living Christ will bring rich blessing and benefit to those under your care.

SOURCES AND CREDITS

INDEX OF SPIRITUAL READINGS